The Colfax County War

Violence and Corruption in Territorial New Mexico

Corey Recko

Number 22 in the A. C. Greene Series

University of North Texas Press
Denton, Texas

Permissions:
University of North Texas Press
1155 Union Circle #311336
Denton, TX 76203-5017

The paper used in this book meets the minimum requirements of the American National Standard for Permanence of Paper for Printed Library Materials, z39.48.1984. Binding materials have been chosen for durability.

Library of Congress Cataloging-in-Publication Data

Names: Recko, Corey, 1974- author.
Title: The Colfax County War : violence and corruption in territorial New Mexico / Corey Recko.
Description: Denton, Texas : University of North Texas Press, [2024] | Series: A. C. Greene series Number 22 | Includes bibliographical references and index.
Identifiers: LCCN 2024012329 (print) | LCCN 2024012330 (ebook) | ISBN 9781574419320 (cloth) | ISBN 9781574419412 (ebook)
Subjects: LCSH: Santa Fe Ring (Political organization)--Corrupt practices. | Land tenure--New Mexico--Colfax County--History--19th century. | Violence--New Mexico--Colfax County--History--19th century. | Maxwell Land Grant (N.M. and Colo.)--History. | New Mexico--History--1848- | BISAC: HISTORY / United States / State & Local / Southwest (AZ, NM, OK, TX) | HISTORY / United States / 19th Century
Classification: LCC F802.C7 R43 2024 (print) | LCC F802.C7 (ebook) | DDC 978.9/2204--dc23/eng/20240403
LC record available at https://lccn.loc.gov/2024012329
LC ebook record available at https://lccn.loc.gov/2024012330

The Colfax County War is Number 22 in the A. C. Greene Series

The electronic edition of this book was made possible by the support of the Vick Family Foundation. Typeset by vPrompt eServices.

To Frederick Nolan (1931–2022)
and Chuck Parsons

Contents

List of

Illustrations and Maps

Acknowledgments

This book has been over sixteen years in the making. During that time I've received assistance from many people. I would like to thank the following, for without them this book wouldn't be possible: Hannah Abelbeck, archivist, Palace of the Governors Photo Archives; Melissa T. Salazar, archives bureau chief, Felicia Lujan, senior archivist, and Dena Hunt, New Mexico State Records Center and Archives; Lenny Silverman, Teddie Moreno, and Cecelia D. Carrasco, library specialists, and Elizabeth Villa, archives specialist, Ld, Reprographics Unit; Stephen J. Hussman, former department head, and Dennis Daily, department head, Archives and Special Collections, New Mexico State University Library; Jim Bradshaw, archivist, the Haley Memorial Library and History Center; Katrina Denman, library assistant for western history, and Peter J. Blodgett, H. Russell Smith Foundation curator of western American history, Huntington Library; Sean Evans, archivist, Cline Library, Northern Arizona University; Betsy Caldwell, reference services coordinator, Indiana Historical Society; Daniel Fink, Newberry Library; Nan J. Card, curator of manuscripts, Rutherford B. Hayes Presidential Center; Jill Tatem, university archivist, Case Western Reserve University; Thomas Vince, Western Reserve Academy; Claudia Ramirez, library archivist, and Danny Gonzalez, public services librarian, El Paso Public Library; Herb Marsh, Henn-Johnson Library and Local History Archives Foundation; Damishia R. Foster and Fred Romanski, archivists, Civilian Records, Textual Archives Services Division, National Archives and Records Administration; Sharon Yates, administrator of the Presbytery of Santa Fe; Mischa Warner and Professor Sydney Van Nort, archivist, City College of New York Archives; Dennie R. Gum, assistant librarian/office manager, Arthur Johnson Memorial Library; Becki Plunkett, special collections archivist/coordinator, State Historical Society of Iowa; Cindy Abel Morris, pictorial archivist, Center for Southwest Research and Special Collections, University of New Mexico; Gregory J. Gill, archivist, New Jersey State Archives; Dorinda Millan, West of the Pecos

Museum director; Benjamin Davis, Linda Davis, and Julia Stafford of the
CS Cattle Company; Daniel Gurule, park manager, Cimarron Canyon State
Park; Candee Rinde of the Cimarron Chamber of Commerce for access to
the old Cimarron jail; Stephanie Scott for scanning a pair of Washington,
DC, newspaper articles; Sandra Duncan Sabourin for the photo of John and
Laura Allison; Ann Oswald for the Stonewall Cemetery information; Len
Gratteri for the Cimarron photographs; Tim Hagaman for sharing a photo
of Melvin Whitson Mills from the TT Hagaman Southwest Collection; and
Reverend Will Steinsiek, NM archivist of the New Mexico Conference of
the United Methodist Church. For getting me countless interlibrary loans,
I'd like to thank Patricia Williams of the Los Angeles Central Library; Sue
Kleme, Eddie Johnson, Tonya Jenkins, Michelle Makkos, Pamela Benjamin,
Melanie Guzman McCarter, and Kelly Ross of the Cleveland Public Library;
and Kathy Jones, adult services librarian, Lisa Ohanian, adult services and
archives librarian, and Derrick Ranostaj, emerging technologies librarian, of
the Hudson Library and Historical Society.

I'd also like to thank Lori Goodloe for creating a map of Cimarron for
this book; Richard Weddle, with whom I've had some informative and enjoy-
able correspondence about Frank W. Angel's investigation; Ed Gooden, who
provided me with important documents related to the Colfax County War;
Kevin McDevitt for the valuable information about the St. James Hotel;
Ron Chrisman, director at UNT Press, and James B. Mills for giving feedback and editing notes on the manuscript; Amy Maddox, managing editor
at UNT Press, for painstakingly editing the manuscript; Joe Alderman,
marketing manager at UNT Press; Sharon Cunningham for information
about the Allison family—particularly Clay and his brother John—and for
reading and giving me helpful feedback on the manuscript; Jim Klaiber
for information about F. J. Tolby's family (his family photographs are
wonderful); Quentin Robinson for Tolby family information and sharing a
copy of a tintype identified as F. J. Tolby; Chuck Hornung for answering
questions about the St. James Hotel and Cimarron, for providing numerous
photographs, and for reading the manuscript and giving valuable feedback;
Reverend Matthew Gary for sharing his F. J. Tolby research; David Caffey
for sharing everything he had copied from the CS Cattle Company archives;

and Gene Lamm, who runs the Old Aztec Mill Museum, for answering many questions about Cimarron and its history and for sharing many photographs from the museum's collection for use in this book. I greatly appreciate the help of Chuck Parsons and his generosity in sending me his Clay Allison research and for critiquing the manuscript. My family has not only given me considerable support, but my magnificent wife, Meg, and wonderful daughters, Gwen and Hanna, have also accompanied me on many research trips and have shown genuine interest in the many museums, historic sites, and cemeteries we've visited.

Finally, I would like to thank the world's foremost authority on the Lincoln County War, Frederick Nolan. It was during a conversation with Fred many years ago in Santa Fe that I told him I was researching Frank Angel's investigation into the troubles in New Mexico but was unsure what the project would turn into. He suggested I focus on the Colfax County War and has been helpful in sharing his own research and putting me in contact with others who were knowledgeable about this topic. Sadly, Fred passed away while I was doing another of many rewrites of the manuscript. I will be forever grateful for his continued support. Fred was an amazing researcher, a prolific writer, a mentor, and a friend. He will be missed.

Introduction

The term *Colfax County War* is most often used to refer to a period of violence and murder in Colfax County, New Mexico, in late 1875 and the fallout from that violence that lasted through the results of a federal investigation in 1878. The name is also sometimes used to describe a long-term dispute over what land was and wasn't public domain in the territory of New Mexico, and specifically much of Colfax County, in the 1870s and 1880s. While the longer-term dispute was a battle between the Maxwell Land Grant Company and squatters who considered the land the company claimed as part of the Maxwell Land Grant to be public domain, the murders in 1875 brought elements of both sides together in a fight against a corrupt group of politicians known as the Santa Fe Ring, making the Colfax County War, in its simplest terms, the citizens in and around Cimarron, New Mexico, versus the Santa Fe Ring.

When New Mexico became part of the United States with the Mexican-American War and the Gadsden Purchase, the territory contained 295 land grants, the largest of these being the Maxwell Land Grant. The land claimed by the Maxwell Land Grant's owners was rich in natural resources such as coal, copper, and gold, but the size and boundaries of the Maxwell Land Grant (as well as other grants) were disputed, with some believing that much of the land was public domain. This led to people settling on land within what others believed to be the boundaries of the grant. Those who settled on this land were fought not only by the land grant owners but also by politicians who tried to use the situation for personal profit and land acquisition.

The fight escalated in late 1875 with the assassination of a prominent citizen who was outspoken against the Santa Fe Ring. In a confession one of the assassins stated that men connected to the Ring had paid to have the man killed. Outrage, civil unrest, and more murders followed. The town of Cimarron alone was the scene of a lynching, a barroom gunfight in the St. James Hotel involving legendary gunman Clay Allison, a nighttime murder of a prisoner, and other killings not related to the political troubles. Despite the murders and allegations that political leaders in the territory planned the assassination that started the violence, the troubles in New Mexico were largely ignored by the federal government. Then, in 1878, two events changed everything. On February 18 a Lincoln County sheriff's posse murdered a young English rancher named John Tunstall, setting off a wave of violence known as the Lincoln County War. In April of that year, a letter came to light that appeared to show that the governor of the territory, Samuel B. Axtell, planned a mass killing of people he considered to be agitators in the Colfax County troubles. Finally, officials in Washington took notice.

Frank W. Angel, an investigator representing both the Departments of Justice and the Interior, went to New Mexico with orders to investigate the violence, murders, and corruption that plagued the territory. The actions taken as a result of Angel's investigation wouldn't end the violence in New Mexico, but it did lead to what many considered to be the end of the Colfax County War, although the legal battles over land grants would continue for years.

Chapter 1

The Maxwell
Land Grant

The territory of New Mexico became part of the United States in 1848 as a result of the Mexican-American War and the Treaty of Guadalupe Hidalgo. New Mexico was officially organized as a territory in 1850 and grew larger with the Gadsden Purchase in 1853.[1] Inside the borders of the new territory were 295 land grants. Of these, 154 were community land grants, meaning the land was public for the good of the community. The remaining 141 were individual, privately owned land grants.[2] According to both the Treaty of Guadalupe Hidalgo and the Gadsden Purchase, land grant owners could keep their grants. The problem was that the grants were handed out by two governments (Spain, then Mexico) over 150 years, and questions of ownership and boundaries arose.[3]

The largest grant was the Maxwell Land Grant, which was originally known as the Beaubien-Miranda Land Grant. It was about 1.7 million aces, with a width averaging forty-five miles and a length of over sixty miles, although the size and boundaries of the grant were in dispute, as will be seen.[4] Charles (sometimes called Carlos) Beaubien, a French-Canadian by birth, was a wealthy merchant in Taos, New Mexico. In 1841 Beaubien, with Guadalupe Miranda, who was the private secretary to New Mexico governor

Manuel Armijo, petitioned the governor for a grant to a large tract of land east of Taos. The reason they gave for applying for the grant was that the area was rich in resources but going to waste because those who lived there were mostly ignorant and not taking advantage of the valuable land. They wanted to develop the land and employ the inhabitants. They were awarded the grant three days after applying. The grant, at 1.7 million acres, was much larger than the 97,424 acres allowed for two individuals under Mexican law (the law allowing 11 leagues, or 48,712 acres per individual). This, along with vague borders, would cause problems in the future.[5]

On June 3, 1844, Charles Beaubien's 13-year-old daughter, María de la Luz, married 25-year-old Lucien B. Maxwell, a trader and trapper who had hunted for expeditions across the West. Soon after marrying Beaubien's daughter, Maxwell became involved in grant business and started a settlement on the Rayado River. In 1858 Lucien Maxwell purchased Guadalupe Miranda's share of the grant and set up a new headquarters on the Cimarron River ten miles north of the Rayado settlement, where the Maxwells built an impressive home in what would become known as Cimarron. When Charles Beaubien died in 1864, Maxwell and his wife not only inherited a piece of the grant but also bought up the rest of the land from the other heirs. The grant's value increased as more people became aware of its fertile ground and natural resources, such as coal, copper, and vast forests that could be used for lumber.[6]

Lucien Maxwell allowed settlers to live on the land in exchange for a portion of what they produced. With the discovery of gold near Elizabethtown, the population on the grant quickly increased, as did the grant's value. Maxwell decided it was time to sell rather than deal with the increased difficulty of managing the grant.[7]

A group led by Jerome B. Chaffee and including United States District Attorney for New Mexico Stephen B. Elkins won the bidding for the grant. Lucien Maxwell was recommended to take the deal by his legal advisor, Thomas B. Catron, who also happened to be a good friend and law partner of Steve Elkins.[8] Elkins and Catron were in the early stages of forming a powerful alliance of men working to advance each other's interests that detractors would coin the Santa Fe Ring. The group went ahead with the deal even though the size of the grant was in question because of the limits set by Mexican law (which the United States would follow since the grant was given out when the territory was part of Mexico). On May 26, 1869, they acquired an option for the land. On December 3 of that year, Secretary of the Interior Jacob D. Cox ruled the grant was 97,424 acres. Despite this being significantly smaller than what Chaffee's group hoped for, the group continued with negotiations and agreed to a new option to purchase the land. However, they were just acting as middlemen for Maxwell and immediately began negotiating the sale of the grant to an English group headed by John Collinson. Because foreigners were not allowed to own land in New Mexico, Collinson's group had three New Mexicans front for them. They were Thomas Rush Spencer, the New Mexican surveyor general; John S. Watts, former chief justice of the territorial supreme court; and William A. Pile, New Mexico's governor.[9] They expected to profit not only from the land's many resources but also by having a train route cross the grant that would connect the eastern United States to California. The option was transferred to the new group on April 30, 1870. The newly formed company, called the Maxwell Land Grant and Railway Company, purchased the land for $1.35 million. At 97,424 acres, that worked out to $13.86 an acre. However, a new survey by William W. Griffin put the grant back at 1.7 million acres. The aforementioned New Mexico surveyor general Thomas Rush Spencer approved the survey.[10] This shows how the group of men who came to be known as the Santa Fe Ring would use positions of power for their own benefit. The grant's new owners behaved as if the grant's size and boundaries matched the Griffin survey while the legal fight continued.

While Lucien and Luz Maxwell and their family relocated to Fort Sumner, New Mexico, where the Maxwells purchased an old army fort for ranching, the Maxwell Land Grant and Railway Company made their headquarters in the mansion Maxwell had built in Cimarron. A group of Dutch financiers from Amsterdam agreed to handle the company's mortgage and $5 million of stock was issued. The plan was to use the money raised to survey, subdivide, and sell the land while also mining the natural resources. To promote the grant and attract settlers, the Maxwell Land Grant and Railway Company hired Alexander P. Sullivan to establish a newspaper, the *Cimarron News*.[11]

Lucien Maxwell's Cimarron mansion, center, circa 1865. This building would become the headquarters of the Maxwell Land Grant and Railway Company. Photographer unknown. Old Aztec Mill Museum, Cimarron, NM.

The company obtained legal opinions from many top lawyers in the nation—including former United States attorney general William A. Evarts and former Confederate secretary of war and secretary of state Judah P. Benjamin—supporting the survey that put the grant at 1.7 million acres.[12] Despite these opinions, in 1871 United States secretary of the interior Columbus Delano ruled the grant was 97,424 acres—twenty-two square leagues—because of acreage limits that didn't allow land grants to exceed eleven square leagues per individual. Since the original grant was given to two people (Charles Beaubien and Guadalupe Miranda), it could not exceed twenty-two square leagues. Delano instructed the Maxwell Land Grant and Railway Company to choose 97,424 acres and ruled that the remainder of the land was public domain. The grant company gained an ally in Washington when Jerome B. Chaffee was elected as Colorado's delegate to Congress 1870. In 1872 they gained more influence in Congress with the election of Stephen B. Elkins as New Mexico's delegate. Both men hoped to use their influence on behalf of Maxwell Land Grant company interests.[13]

Meanwhile, the company had to deal with the growing problem that many settlers on the grant did not recognize the company's ownership of the land. Some sided with Delano's decision and fought the Maxwell Land Grant and Railway Company on the grounds that the company didn't own all of the land it laid claim to. Siding with those who legitimately challenged the size and boundaries of the Maxwell Land Grant were people who held a then more traditional view of the frontier as public domain. They stood against those who understood that grant land in New Mexico, because of its roots in Spanish and Mexican law, was private property. This had been a problem for Lucien Maxwell when he owned the grant. Maxwell had come to agreements with settlers by accepting produce from their farms and charging miners a small fee for mining on his property, and he did not press the issue with those who refused to recognize his title to the land. The Maxwell Land Grant and Railway Company honored the agreements Maxwell had made. However, to those who did not have agreements with Maxwell, the company sent out notices to make arrangements or to vacate the property. Most of the settlers who received these notices ignored them, so Stephen B. Elkins, attorney for the company, filed ejectment proceedings against them.[14]

On October 27, 1870, the conflict over the grant boundaries led to a riot in Elizabethtown that resulted in miners setting fire to the home of the justice of the peace and burning down two large buildings on the town's main street. Troops were brought in from Cimarron to stop the riot, but by the time they arrived, local citizens already had brought an end to the outbreak.

Another riot in Elizabethtown broke out in April 1871, when an armed mob took control of Maxwell company property. The armed miners did eventually leave the scene but made it known that they would not vacate their claims until it was proved the company's title was valid.[15]

Elizabethtown, circa 1868. Photographer unknown. Maxwell Land Grant Company Photograph Collection, Negative #155027, Center for Southwest Research, University of New Mexico, Albuquerque, NM.

Elizabethtown, known as E-town, had been founded just a few years earlier. Copper brought soldiers from Fort Union to the area. In 1866 the men found gold and soon people began to populate the area and make their claims. The town was incorporated in 1868 and named Elizabethtown after Elizabeth Moore, the daughter of John H. Moore, one of the town's founders. Soon after, miners began calling the place E-town. Elizabethtown grew rapidly, reaching a population somewhere between three thousand and seven thousand people (depending on the source). It had approximately one hundred buildings at the time, including stores, hotels, dance halls, saloons, a brewery, and many homes. In 1870 E-town was named the county seat of the newly formed Colfax County (created in 1869), a distinction it held for only two years because the population soon plummeted as the mines dried up. The once booming town quickly saw its population drop to about only one hundred.[16]

On November 11, 1872, the Maxwell Land Grant and Railway Company appointed William Raymond Morley as executive officer. Morley, who would go on to play a big role in the coming troubles, was born in Hampden County, Massachusetts, on September 15, 1846. His father died in 1853 and

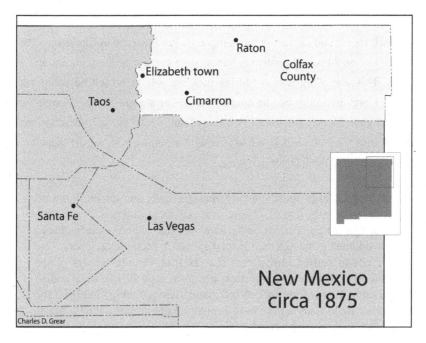

Map of northeast New Mexico. Map by Dr. Charles David Grear.

his mother in 1857, so young William and a brother were sent to Iowa to be raised by his aunt and uncle on their farm. In early 1864, at the age of 17, Morley lied about his age and enlisted in the Union Army. He served through the end of the war as part of Company F of the 9th Regiment of Iowa Volunteer Infantry. In 1866 Morley enrolled in the State University of Iowa, where he studied engineering. Morley never earned a degree but worked his way into the profession when he took a job as a land surveyor for the Iowa Northern Railroad. During this time Morley, who went by Raymond or Ray, had an ongoing courtship with Ada McPherson, who would also figure prominently in what would become known as the Colfax County War. Ada was born on August 26, 1852, in Winterset, Iowa. Described by her daughter as "a golden-haired sprightly girl with musical talent," Ada attended the State University of Iowa, where she and William met. Shortly after William Morley took the job as executive officer of the Maxwell Land Grant and Railway Company he and Ada were married. In 1874 their first child, Agnes, was born.

As part of the incentive for his new job, Morley was given the use of the two back rooms and kitchen in the company's headquarters in Cimarron—the former Lucien Maxwell mansion—along with the use of three horses and a buggy. This was a big reason Morley took the job, as he felt he could ask Ada to marry him now that he could provide her a good home. Though the contract gave Morley the use of two rooms and a kitchen, later descriptions from Agnes show the Morleys had access to an entire wing of the mansion. Agnes described the interior this way:

> I recall four large square pianos, massive beds and chairs, huge oil paintings in gilt frames. There was silver, and crystal, and fine china. One room was set aside as a museum where were gathered those oddments that rich men seem disposed to accumulate. There were hundreds of stuffed birds—rare species from remote corners of the world. My most vivid recollection, however, is of the two royal Indian tigers that guarded the foot of the grand staircase which led from the entrance hall. Many a time have I mounted one of those jungle beasts and galloped away to adventure.[17]

At the time Morley took the job, the Maxwell Land Grant and Railway Company was in financial trouble so severe that in 1872 the company took out two mortgages on the grant. They received some help in going after squatters when Thomas Catron was appointed United States attorney by President Ulysses S. Grant, but this wasn't enough to turn the finances around. The year 1872 was also when Stephen B. Elkins became president of the company. In 1873 his good friend Catron was named as a director. Under Elkins the company's money troubles continued.[18]

The financial difficulties worsened as the United States entered an economic depression in late 1873 that lasted until 1878. It began when the Northern Pacific Railroad ran out of money, causing the closure of Jay Cooke's bank, its biggest shareholder. The bank's failure led to what became known as the Panic of 1873.[19] The panic caused Elias Brevoort to call off plans to run a railroad over the Maxwell Land Grant. The Atchison, Topeka, and Santa Fe Railway (AT&SF) Corporation was also interested in running a line across the Maxwell Land Grant and willing to become a partner in the Maxwell Land Grant and Railway Company. William Morley, who in

William Raymond Morley, circa 1880. Photographer unknown. Norman Cleaveland Papers, Image #00250002, Rio Grande Historical Collections, New Mexico State University Archives and Special Collections, Las Cruces, NM.

October 1873 would have vice president added to his title, met with Stephen B. Elkins in Washington, DC, to discuss the plan. From Washington, Elkins and Morley traveled to Holland to meet with the company's bondholders to discuss the AT&SF proposal and the state of the company. The company's problems continued when the deal with AT&SF fell through.[20]

Through the many challenges, William Morley worked hard to promote the resources of the grant to attract settlers. For this purpose, he created a map of New Mexico that included information on the territory's resources and various land grants. As he was now the manager, his name also appeared as editor of the company's newspaper, the *Cimarron News*.[21]

Despite Morley's efforts, he could not bring in much money. Because of the depression, many of the newcomers to the grant who were willing to pay rent could only do so in produce. And this represented only a tiny number of the people who were on the grant, since most refused to give the Maxwell Land Grant and Railway Company any amount of money or goods because they did not believe the company owned the land. The result was that Morley failed to get anything out of the vast majority of those who occupied the land. The company demanded that those who wouldn't pay needed to vacate, but since the squatters did not believe the company's claim to the land to be legitimate, they stayed right where they were.[22]

Multiple "squatters' clubs" were organized, including one in Cimarron, to defend squatters' rights and oppose grant company interests. The Cimarron Squatters' Club's stated goal was to raise money to sue the Maxwell Land Grant and Railway Company to "test the validity" of the company's title to the land.[23] To deal with the legal problems facing the company, Morley asked Frank Springer, a lawyer and former classmate of his, to come from Iowa and work for the company as an attorney and also to help run the *Cimarron News*.

Frank Springer was born to a prominent family on July 17, 1848, in Wapello, Iowa. His father, Francis, had been a lawyer, judge, and member of the Iowa Senate. At the age of 13, Frank Springer entered the Baptist College in Burlington, and a year later he enrolled at the State University of Iowa. He graduated with a bachelor of philosophy degree in 1867. During his time in school, Springer developed an interest in science that stayed with him throughout his life. As his interest in science grew, he separated himself from organized religion. The only thing that kept Springer from choosing a career in science was the lack of money to be made. Even so, he never lost this interest and began what would become a substantial fossil collection. Deciding he wanted more money than a scientific career could provide, Springer studied law. He read law under Burlington attorney Henry Strong and briefly returned to the State University of Iowa to study at the university's law school. Springer began to practice law under Henry Strong in 1869 and in 1870 was appointed assistant to the district attorney for the First Judicial District of Iowa. In 1872 his family suffered a loss when his younger brother Warren drowned in the Iowa River while hunting.

Frank Springer, circa 1870. Photograph by Montfort and Hill Studio.
Negative #45480, Palace of the Governors Photo Archives, Santa Fe, NM
(NMHM/DCA).

In his friend Ray Morley's offer, Frank Springer saw a promising
opportunity, so he accepted and went to work for the Maxwell Land Grant
and Railway Company while also opening a law office on the north side of
the Cimarron Plaza and purchasing land for a ranch. As Springer acquainted
himself with New Mexico law, he received guidance from Thomas Catron.[24]

Shortly after Springer arrived in the territory, his new employer's continuing conflict with squatters led to more trouble as the Cimarron Squatters' Club threw their support behind a man named John Lynch, who had been living on land the Maxwell Land Grant and Railway Company sold to Henry M. Porter and George M. Carpenter. When Lynch was found guilty of trespassing but refused to vacate, the squatters' club backed him up. Despite his initial refusal to go, Lynch did peacefully leave the house and land owned by Carpenter and Porter. John Crowley, on behalf of Porter and Carpenter, moved into the house. Crowley and another man, William Parker, were occupying the house on the night of May 1, 1873, when two men opened fire on the building. Crowley and Parker, awakened by the gunfire, quickly grabbed their arms and returned fire. One of the men outside called out that he was hit, and while the other shooter fled, Crowley and Parker went to help the wounded man, who turned out to be Elizabethtown founder John Moore. Moore, who would die from his wounds, did not disclose the reason for his attack, but it was believed that harsh words Crowley had made about the squatters' club prompted it.[25]

Frank Springer and Ray Morley had many detractors as a result of their positions with the Maxwell Land Grant and Railway Company. One influential enemy they made was rancher Clay Allison—a leader among area ranchers. The reason for Allison's animosity toward them is unclear. While it could have been as simple as Allison supporting the squatters Springer and Morley worked to evict, Allison's political support for the ruling clique, such as Stephen Elkins, undercuts this theory, as Elkins was no friend of the squatters. Another possibility is that Morley and Springer's positions as editors of the *Cimarron News*, in which they were critical of Elkins and other incumbent politicians that Allison supported, drew Allison's ire. Whatever the reasons, the relationship was so bad that, according to a Morley family story, one night when Allison rode into Cimarron "shooting up the town," William Morley, worried that Allison came looking for him, went into hiding. While in his hideout, he missed the birth of his daughter Agnes.[26]

William Morley brought in some revenue for the company when he worked out a deal to supply beef to the Ute and Apache Indian Agency at Cimarron. For a time the company profited from this deal. Then, in 1875,

Cimarron, circa 1877. The issue of rations to local Native Americans at the Aztec Mill. In the background on the left is the Maxwell Land Grant Company Headquarters and home of William and Ada Morley (formerly Lucien Maxwell's house). To the right is the St. James Hotel (also known as Lambert's Saloon). Photographer unknown. Old Aztec Mill Museum, Cimarron, NM.

the tribes received spoiled beef and protested. Shots were fired and, during the encounter, Juan Barela, who was described as a minor chief, was killed. The US government took steps to make the situation right and supply fresh meat, but the Maxwell Land Grant and Railway Company would lose this revenue stream as the agency was discontinued the following year and the Utes and Apaches were slowly moved to new reservations.[27]

Chapter 2

The Santa Fe Ring at Work

The year 1875 began for the territory of New Mexico with a bill for statehood. Actually, the bill, H.R. 2418, had passed the House of Representatives on May 21, 1874, but with the new year it, along with a bill for statehood for the territory of Colorado, had yet to be voted on by the Senate. The Senate passed both bills on February 24, 1875. However, the Senate added amendments to both bills so they were returned to the House. Colorado's bill came up first and passed on March 3, 1875. Then the New Mexico bill came up for a vote. It failed to get the needed two-thirds to pass, with a final vote of 154 to 85 (with 49 abstaining), which was just short of the two-thirds needed at 63.9 percent.[1]

It has been written that the reason the vote failed was a handshake. According to this story, the bill had enough votes to pass until a blunder by Stephen Elkins. It was said that before the vote, Julius Caesar Burrows, a representative from Michigan, gave a speech on a different bill in which he said many unkind words about the South and the rebellion that caused the Civil War. Elkins had been talking to friends in the lobby and did not hear the speech, but reentered the chamber just after Burrows finished and shook Burrows's hand. Supposedly, many southern representatives saw this and changed their votes.[2] The *Congressional Record*, however, does not support this claim. A look at the votes shows it was mostly Republicans and northern representatives that voted for Colorado's admission to the Union but not New Mexico's. Of the one hundred sixty-four "Yes" votes for Colorado that changed to "No" for New Mexico, only four were from those representing former Confederate states. Another ten representatives who voted in favor of Colorado's admission abstained from the New Mexico vote. Only one of these representatives was from a former Confederate state.[3] The reality is that several reasons kept the territory from becoming a state, including that many New Mexicans did not speak English, the lack of public schools and high illiteracy rate, and the small population spread over a vast area.[4] The violence that would soon erupt would do further harm to the cause.

While Elkins was fighting for statehood in Congress, Maxwell Land Grant and Railway Company executive officer William Morley was reconsidering a decision he had made to leave the company. In November 1874 Morley resigned, but the resignation was not to take effect until May 5, 1875. Morley's poor health may have been the reason for his resignation, as his surveying work had been difficult and led to bouts of rheumatism (a term that covers a range of medical problems usually associated with pain and stiffness in the muscles and joints). Despite his poor health, Morley changed his mind and stayed with the company.[5]

One reason Morley withdrew his resignation might have been to save the company from Elkins and Catron. His role with the company gave him a close-up view of the workings of the Santa Fe Ring, and Morley, instead of joining them, which he was certainly in a position to do, opposed their scheming. Morley's grandson, Norman Cleaveland, later wrote that he believed that "the Santa Fe Ring was attempting to gain control of the Grant."[6] In exposing and opposing the Santa Fe Ring, and with a newspaper to aid his cause, Morley could help prevent the grant from falling under Ring control.

In its simplest terms, the Santa Fe Ring (a name given by its detractors) was a group of powerful, mostly Republican, New Mexicans—including politicians, judges, lawyers, and business owners—whose goal was mutual economic gain that was mainly obtained by federal patronage and control over the territorial government. This included land grabs, with Ring lawyers and politicians using the confusion over grant titles and boundaries to gain land for themselves. Not a formal organization, the Ring, led by Stephen Elkins and Thomas Catron, was simply a group of individuals who shared a desire for power and wealth, had similar economic and political interests, and cooperated for mutual gain. Another powerful ally was Judge Joseph Palen, who used the courts to benefit Ring interests.

Joseph G. Palen was born in Palenville, New York, in 1812. After attending a few colleges, he studied law in the office of Ambrose L. Jordan in Hudson, New York, and went on to practice law there. In 1861 he was appointed postmaster of Hudson and occupied that post until his appointment as chief justice of New Mexico in 1869.[7]

Joseph G. Palen, circa 1869. Photographer unknown. Donald S. Dreesen Collection of Pictures of Prominent New Mexicans, Center for Southwest Research, University of New Mexico.

Stephen Benton Elkins was born in Perry County, Ohio, in 1841. His family moved to Westport, Missouri. Elkins attended the Masonic College in Lexington, Missouri, and then the University of Missouri at Columbia, where he graduated from in 1860. He served in the Union Army early in the Civil War, reaching the rank of captain. Elkins moved to Mesilla, New Mexico, in 1864, where he was admitted to the bar, opened a law practice, and was elected to the territorial legislative assembly. He moved to Santa Fe in 1865. Soon after, the fast-rising Elkins was appointed district attorney for the territory, then appointed to be New Mexico's attorney general, and then United States district attorney for New Mexico. During this period Elkins was given the nickname "Smooth Steve." He married in 1866. His wife, Sarah, died in 1872, leaving Stephen with two young daughters.[8]

Stephen Benton Elkins. Photograph by M. Brady, date unknown. Negative #091328, Palace of the Governors Photo Archives, Santa Fe, NM (NMHM/DCA).

Thomas Catron became directly involved in Maxwell Land Grant cases when he and Stephen Elkins became law partners in January 1874.[9] The two close friends were very different but worked well together. Edgar Walz, Catron's brother-in-law, once said of the men, "I have often . . . heard it said that if one asked Mr. Elkins for a favor, he would shake you by the hand, smile on you, pat you on the back and ask you to come again, but he would never grant your wish; that if you asked Catron for a favor, he would bluster, take your head nearly off, but give you what you asked for if it was a reasonable request."[10]

Thomas Benton Catron was born in Lafayette County, Missouri, in 1840. He enrolled in the Masonic College in Lexington in 1857, where he met Steve Elkins. Catron then went to the University of Missouri at Columbia in 1860, the same class as Elkins. Shortly after graduating Catron enlisted in the Confederate Army and fought in numerous battles. Following the war Tom Catron returned to Missouri to study law but was disbarred there due to his service in the Confederate Army, so he relocated to Santa Fe, New Mexico, in 1866. That same year he was appointed district attorney for the Third Judicial District in Mesilla, even though he had not yet been admitted to the bar. He was admitted to the bar the next year. Catron was appointed attorney general of New Mexico in 1869 and served in that post until his appointment as United States attorney for the territory in 1872.[11]

Morley and Springer almost lost one of the tools used to fight the Santa Fe Ring when the *Cimarron News* suspended publication in November of 1874, but a month later they, along with Will Dawson of the *Elizabethtown Press and Telegraph*, revived the paper by consolidating it with the *Press and Telegraph*. The paper, now called the *Cimarron News and Press*, was no longer under Maxwell Land Grant and Railway Company control, and the paper's editors—Morley, Springer, and Dawson—vowed to take a neutral position on land grant questions.[12]

Spring marked the arrival of Mary McPherson, the mother of William Morley's wife, Ada, to Colfax County. McPherson would go on to play an important role in bringing attention to the coming violence and corruption in New Mexico. Born Mary Elizabeth Tibbles in 1831 to a large family in Marietta in southeast Ohio, McPherson was a widow and a mother of three

Thomas Benton Catron. Date and photographer unknown. Author's collection.

daughters. Two of her daughters were grown and the third, Mary, was about 4 years old when she arrived with her mother in Cimarron. McPherson immediately became interested in local politics and was influenced heavily by the Reverend Franklin J. Tolby, a local Methodist preacher who was very vocal in his opposition to the Santa Fe Ring.[13]

Passionate over what she observed, Mary McPherson wrote a letter to officials in Washington about the lawlessness and corruption (i.e., the Santa Fe Ring) in the territory. When McPherson's daughter Ada heard about the letter, she rushed to the Cimarron Post Office to retrieve it. The mail drop box was simply a box on a table, so Ada Morley found her mother's letter in the box and took it. The postmaster, John B. McCulloch, reported the incident. Based on McCulloch's testimony, US Attorney Catron had Ada Morley indicted for mail theft.[14]

Ada Morley, circa 1873. Photographer unknown. Norman Cleaveland Papers, image #00250004, Rio Grande Historical Collections, New Mexico State University Archives and Special Collections, Las Cruces, NM.

Frank Springer, when questioned later about the charges, said that he approached Dr. Robert H. Longwill, a Colfax County probate judge and known Santa Fe Ring supporter, to ask him to "use his influence to stop" the prosecution and, assuming they were going after Ada Morley because of differences with her husband, gave his opinion that a man shouldn't be fought "by attacking his family." Longwill promised to do what he could but, according to Springer, added that William Morley "ought to stop attacking Elkins through the newspaper." Springer went to Santa Fe and there saw another influential Santa Fe Ring member, Cimarron attorney Melvin W. Mills. Mills told Springer that they were determined to indict Ada Morley.[15]

Besides the contention that they were trying to punish her husband, another possible reason for going after Ada Morley was given by Asa F. Middaugh. In a sworn statement Middaugh said that he had a conversation with Thomas Catron about the Morley indictment. According to his deposition, "Catron declared that Mrs Morley had insulted him by taking away a certain buggy at a time when said Catron wanted to use it and that said Morley had been throwing mud at him, and that he—said Catron—had a chance to get even now, and he would be a fool if he did not take advantage of it." While Morley was never prosecuted because the indictment was never served, the fear of arrest hung over her because the indictment was never dropped, either. Whatever the motives behind the indictment, had Catron realized he was making a powerful enemy in Ada's mother, Mary McPherson, he may not have pursued the issue. But Morley was indicted and McPherson would come back to haunt Catron.[16]

While Ring powers made sure Ada Morley was indicted for mail theft, soon after it was rumored that they used their influence to prevent the indictment of an ally involved in a much more serious crime. On a Sunday evening on May 30, 1875, Juan Francisco "Pancho" Griego, who had spent some time in the New Mexico Infantry, was dealing a game of monte in the St. James Hotel barroom (formerly known as Lambert's Saloon) in Cimarron. Soldiers from Fort Union were gathered around the table betting when a disagreement arose over a bet and one of the soldiers grabbed some of the money on the table. Griego quickly scooped up the rest, then sprung back from the table while the soldiers surrounded him and were said to have grabbed at him—likely trying to take back the rest of the money. Griego drew a pistol and Bowie knife and the soldiers turned and ran as he quickly stabbed Private Patrick Gaitley and opened fire, shooting Private Michael Carrol through the thigh and killing Private Benjamin Sheahan. Pancho Griego then ran out of the building and went into hiding. Patrick Gaitley, the man Griego had stabbed, later died from his wounds.[17]

Griego soon returned to town, surrendered, and was taken before the justice of the peace who, according to Frank Springer, was a clerk in Mills's law office. Springer claimed the justice of the peace consulted with Longwill and Mills before he bound Griego over on $1,000 bail to await the action of the grand jury. While out on bail, Griego worked for both the campaigns of Robert Longwill for reelection as probate judge and Melvin Mills, who was running against Frank Springer for a seat on the territorial legislative assembly. These close ties between Griego and alleged Ringites were viewed with suspicion.[18]

As outrage over this and the Santa Fe Ring was building, there was a change in the governorship of the territory. Marsh Giddings, who had been the governor of New Mexico since 1871, died on June 3, 1875. Appointed to replace him was Samuel B. Axtell.[19]

Samuel Beach Axtell was born on October 14, 1819, in Franklin County, Ohio, near Columbus. He attended Oberlin College and then finished his schooling at Western Reserve College in Hudson, Ohio. In 1840 he married Adaline S. Williams, and in 1843 they moved to Mount Clemens, Michigan, where Axtell passed the bar and established a law practice. The couple, with their two children, moved to what would soon become Amador County, California, in 1851. There Axtell practiced law, invested in mining, and became involved in politics. The family settled in San Francisco in 1860, where Samuel Axtell practiced law. By 1860 they had four children, although the youngest died that same year. Samuel Axtell was elected to Congress as a Democrat in 1866 and 1868, then he switched to the Republican Party. In 1874 President Ulysses S. Grant appointed Axtell the governor of the territory of Utah.[20]

Samuel Beach Axtell as governor of Utah. Photograph by Charles R. Savage, 1874. PH 1700 1030, Brigham Young University Library, Provo, UT.

Axtell's first action as Utah's governor was to give George Q. Cannon a certificate of election as delegate for the territory in the United States House of Representatives. The previous governor, George L. Woods, refused to certify the election of Cannon because of accusations that his certificate of naturalization was forged and he was not a US citizen. The claim was false. The real reason behind the refusal was that Cannon was a Mormon. When Axtell gave Cannon the certificate of election, a large anti-Mormon segment of Utah's population became angry with Axtell because, in their view, he was doing the church's bidding. Detractors gave Axtell the nickname Bishop. Samuel Axtell stated his position: "I am determined to be a governor, not of a section, but of the whole people." The divide between the Mormons and those against them was so great that anyone who wasn't against the Mormons was seen as being for only their interests. Axtell was attacked in the newspapers, and a consistent stream of demands for his resignation or removal came into Washington. Instead of supporting Axtell in Utah, President Grant chose to make the problem go away by appointing Axtell governor of New Mexico after New Mexico governor Marsh Giddings died. Axtell accepted Grant's offer. He officially resigned as the governor or Utah on June 20, and on July 30 Samuel B. Axtell was sworn in as the governor of the territory of New Mexico.[21]

The conflicts over land grants and the influence of the Santa Fe Ring were heating up in the summer of 1875. The anger over the Maxwell Land Grant's disputed size and boundaries was compounded by charges that the Santa Fe Ring controlled the courts in New Mexico. Adding fuel to the fire were two letters that appeared in the *New York Sun* that were very critical of those in power in New Mexico.[22] Under the headline "The Territory of Elkins," the first letter, written on June 2 and published on July 5, was inspired by the nomination by the New Mexico Republican Convention of Stephen B. Elkins to again run as candidate for delegate to Congress. The letter began with a little New Mexico history and then turned into a partisan attack on Elkins and his law partner, Thomas B. Catron. The anonymous writer opined that Elkins and Catron had benefited greatly since Joseph Palen and Hezekiah S. Johnson—who was also allegedly connected to the Santa Fe Ring—were named to the New Mexico Supreme Court. The correspondent made some serious charges, including that Catron would have people indicted to pressure them to vote for Elkins.[23]

Moving on from Catron and Elkins, the New Mexican took issue with how bills were passed in the territory, claiming that instead of debating bills on the legislative assembly floor, arguments were made off the record in the private offices of Ring members during recesses. According to the correspondent, "immediately following some of these recesses measures were passed in the

Ring interest which will darken the pages of New Mexican history for long years." One example of such a bill was what the writer called "the infamous chuzas law." Though gambling was illegal in the territory, the law made an exception for chuzas (a roulette-like game). Soon after, during which time chuzas had become extremely popular, it was ruled by a court decision to still be illegal. The correspondent reported that hundreds were indicted for playing the game and alleged that spies had been making lists of the players. Ring lawyers, the writer claimed, "pocketed thousands in the way of court and prosecuting attorneys' fees." In another example, one the author called the "most oppressive act of all," the anonymous correspondent took aim at a law that allowed persons "to bring a suit in any county of the judicial district in which either he or the defendant resides and five days' notice, either personal or served by leaving a copy at the defendant's house, whether he or his family are at home or not, constitutes legal service." The writer pointed out how isolated and spread out many in the territory were, especially ranchers who were often away from their homes for long periods of time while tending to their herds, and commented that, "it will be readily seen that in many cases it is simply impossible for a party sued to appear and defend his case, or employ an attorney, for want of time, before judgment is rendered by default." The concerned citizen opined, "The effect of the law is that if any one opposes the Ring, he is liable at any moment to have his property levied on by the Sheriff and sold under a judgment, the existence of which he never knew." The author accused the New Mexico press of being subservient to the Ring but expressed some hope that the coming elections would bring change for the better.[24]

Following this anonymous letter was a letter written by Simeon H. Newman, former editor of the *Las Vegas Weekly Mail*.[25] It ran under the head-line "A Most Audacious Ring." Newman stated, "Elkins and Catron have done all and more than all of what that correspondent has accused them, as hundreds and thousands of the best citizens of both parties in the Territory are ready to testify; but they would long since have been overthrown and driven from the country, were it not that they are supported in every political measure by Joseph G. Palen." Of Palen Newman opined, "The record he has made for himself during his six years' reign is enough to damn any man to an eternity of infamy." He added that many New Mexicans were lobbying to have Palen removed so as to rid themselves of the judge "and the vampires which surround him." Newman made more accusations against the Santa Fe Ring, including a claim that Palen was able to have some attorneys who opposed him disbarred. Simeon Newman closed with, "For a full corroboration of all herein set forth I refer to any prominent citizen of New Mexico, of either political party, who is not directly or indirectly connected with the Ring, and am prepared to produce affidavits from the best men in the Territory to sustain not only these charges, but a thousand more equally as damaging."[26] While some of his attack was partisan and the Ring was comprised mostly of Republicans, there were both Republicans and Democrats who opposed the Santa Fe Ring.

Chapter 3

Franklin J. Tolby

Another anti-Ring force stirring up the emotions of citizens was 33-year-old Reverend Franklin J. Tolby. Born into a large family in Hendricks County, Indiana, on September 26, 1841, Frank Tolby's given name was Benjamin Franklin. Why and when he changed it to Franklin James is unknown. Tolby was a member of the Indiana Infantry during the American Civil War. On March 10, 1870, he married Mary Elizabeth Russell. Their first child, Rachel, was born in 1871. That same year, Tolby was admitted, on trial, to the North-West Indiana Conference of the Methodist Episcopal Church. He was on the Pine Grove Circuit in 1871, then the Brooke Circuit in 1872, and then Morocco in 1873. It was in Morocco, Indiana, that Tolby's second child, Grace, was born on November 22, 1873.[1]

Tolby was transferred to a new post in New Mexico. The area assigned to him included Cimarron, Elizabethtown, and "other adjacent places."[2] About two months after receiving the assignment, on January 29, 1874, he wrote his sister from the family's new home in Cimarron, New Mexico, a place he quickly developed a great appreciation for. "We are now living in our own house, are reasonably well and very comfortably situated. Our house is built of adobes, or sun-dried bricks; in this dry climate these adobe houses are not only comfortable but substantial and beautiful. Our house contains five rooms and a hall. We are well pleased with the country and shall, perhaps, make it our home. We are kindly received by the people, and have pleasant neighbors." He described the area this way: "The roads are nearly always good. Grass sustains live stock [*sic*] all the year round, and the people keep immense herds of cattle and flocks of sheep. . . . The mountains are high; one in sight of our town is thirteen thousand feet high. . . . The people generally appear healthy and strong, and those who have lived here three or four years seem to think that there are few countries equal to it." Tolby saw tremendous growth for his new home in the future, writing, "Cimarron is destined to be the leading city of New Mexico," and a bright future for his work as well:

> Our church's prospects are favorable. I do not recollect that I have, at any time, had stronger hope of success. The Spanish language is easily learned. I expect to be able to preach in Spanish by next new-year's day. . . . I hope father is well. If I succeed here as well as I hope to do, I shall be able to help him materially; and, in any case, I shall always be ready to divide with him. . . . Rachie tells me to write to grand-pa that she and Grace are fat and rosy; and that she "loves him fifteen pounds." . . . Rachie is a big, healthy girl; but Gracie is a very much larger child, at the same age, and has never been sick an hour in her life. . . . Rachie has just said that if grand-pa would come here, she would go to him and would kiss him. . . . Your brother, Frank.[3]

Cimarron, circa 1872. Photographer unknown. Norman Cleaveland Papers, image #00250172, Rio Grande Historical Collections, New Mexico State University Archives and Special Collections, Las Cruces, NM.

While New Mexico Missions superintendent Thomas Harwood expressed some pessimism about Tolby's assignment, saying the "Americans" in Colfax County were not very religious, [4] Tolby was full of optimism. On April 7, 1874, Tolby sent his niece a letter in which he told of his excitement to have already "organized church of five members and a Sunday School which has numbered as high as fifty." Franklin Tolby went on to again expressed his love of New Mexico as he described a country rich in natural resources:

A large portion of the surface of this territory is mountainous; and many of the mountains are full of silver, iron, copper, and coal, gold exists in large quantities in the Moreno Mountains which are near us. I preach once in two weeks in the Moreno mining camp. . . . In some parts of the territory, fruits can be produced as nowhere else on this side of the Pacific coast. In the Mesilla valley, a root graft planted ten years ago is now an apple tree twelve inches in diameter and yields forty bushels of apples. In the valley of the Rio Grande, we produce wine as good, perhaps, as any produced in France. Grapes flourish in many parts of the Rio Grande valley; of this I am assured by Hon. J. G. Palen, Chief Justice of this territory. . . . Any man can find in one part or another of this territory what he wants in the way of a country.

Having his oldest daughter, three-year-old Rachel, talking to him as he finished the letter, the happy father wrote in the margins, "It would amuse you to hear Rachie speak Spanish words. Rachie has just kissed me, saying that she kissed me instead of kissing aunt Sat. because she could not kiss her. She now tells me to write, 'come here aunt Sat. and then "I will kiss you"'" [5]

Tolby again wrote to his niece on July 29, 1874, to let her know he and his family were doing well "notwithstanding Indian hostilities." The hostilities referred to were part of what's known as the Red River War, a yearlong conflict between the United States and the Kiowa, Comanche, Southern Cheyenne, and Arapaho tribes. The Native American tribes were unhappy with the United States government for failure to live up to promises made as part of the 1867 Treaty of Medicine Lodge. Though most of the fight happened east of New Mexico, in July of 1874, the tribes made attacks in the territory. [6] While the war never reached Cimarron, it did hit the surrounding area. Tolby wrote, "They have killed about thirty of our people, and have driven off many horses and mules; but we think that we have them now,

Tintype purportedly showing Franklin James Tolby. Date and photographer unknown. The above photo was identified as Tolby by a niece (who never met him) and passed down in her family. Tintype image is reversed here to show original view. Courtesy of Quentin Robinson.

under control. I furnished dispatches to the *Inter-Ocean* in which you may learn particulars." The *Inter-Ocean* was a Chicago newspaper that published Tolby's letter on July 14, 1874. His letter to his niece continued:

The Indians, resident in our (Colfax) County, remain friendly and assisted us in the war. We feel comparatively safe now, and hope that we shall have no further trouble with the Indians who recently made war on our country. . . . For several days, we lived in apprehension of an attack on any evening or morning; at such times, they make their attacks, usually. . . . One evening when we had put the children in bed and Mary had lain down by them, and when I was about ready to extinguish the light in our room, it was discovered that I had forgotten to bring into the room as usual, a certain weapon of defense; Rachie thought that would not do, and said, "Papa, if you do not bring in your 'volver, the first thing you know you will see that some big Indian will get your girls."[7]

In 1875 Tolby was reappointed to the Cimarron circuit and assigned an assistant, O. P. McMains, who quickly became part of the local community. Tolby became an advocate for the Mohuache Utes and Jicarilla Apaches. While both tribes faced the threat of removal from their homes with the possible closure of the Cimarron Indian Reservation after the conflict over spoiled beef, Tolby fought to keep them in Colfax County—a fight that would be lost. Frank Tolby, whom Reverend Thomas Harwood called "a rising man, bold and fearless in the pulpit and out of it," and who Frank Springer described as "a man of ability and rather free in talking about men and their acts," also became an outspoken critic of the Santa Fe Ring. Cimarron resident and store owner Henry Porter later wrote that Tolby "took quite a lively interest against the methods of the *Santa Fe Ring* and quite openly denounced them."[8]

As the fall term of court began in Cimarron, the seat of Colfax County, Tolby did more than speak out against the Santa Fe Ring; he gave testimony in front of the grand jury against someone who had been campaigning for Ring candidates during the summer. Tolby had witnessed Pancho Griego's fight at the St. James Hotel in May when Griego wounded one man and killed two others. Tolby testified against Griego, but it did no good, as the grand jury declined to charge Griego with any crimes. To many Griego escaping indictment looked like the Santa Fe Ring at work. Griego had been a Ring ally and was working for both Longwill's campaign for reelection as probate judge and for the campaign of Mills, who was running against Frank Springer for a seat on the territorial legislative assembly. He worked to bring them the Native New Mexican vote. What influence those associated with the Ring had on the grand jury is not known, but Springer claimed that Cipriano Lara told him that William Breeden and Thomas Catron had promised him that if he and Griego would use "all their influence with the Mexicans in favor of the ticket of Elkins and Longwill, his friend Griego should not suffer."[9] Suffer he did not. Francisco Griego was a free man.

Another case heard at the fall term of court was for the eviction of the Morleys from the Maxwell house, the result of the Maxwell Land Grant and Railway Company's financial troubles. Unable to pay their taxes, their headquarters in Cimarron was sold at a sheriff's auction in May 1875. The house was divided in two parts, east and west, and sold that way, with the western half being purchased by Henry Lambert and the eastern, where the Morleys were living, by Melvin Mills. While New Mexico law allowed for a redemption period in which the company could pay the back taxes and reclaim the property, Mills wanted immediate use of his new property and sued to evict the Morleys. A summons was left for William Morley at the home on August 20 while he was absent, but he received it in time to appear at the September term of court. The case came before Judge Henry Waldo, who ruled in favor of Mills. Morley appealed the ruling to the New Mexico Supreme Court, who would rule against him the next January. Morley's daughter, however, remembers living in the house past this time, meaning either the Maxwell Land Grant and Railway Company regained the property or the Morleys rented from Mills after the decision against them.[10]

The Santa Fe Ring gained victories when, on Monday, September 6, Robert Longwill was reelected probate judge, Melvin Mills was reelected to the Territorial Legislature, defeating Frank Springer, and Stephen B. Elkins was reelected to Congress. There are claims that, unbeknownst to Elkins— who was still in Holland during the election—his reelection was the result of fraud perpetrated by his supporters. The election was contested and the courts ruled in Elkins's favor.[11] If his victory was because of fraud, this would be another example of the control the corrupt group of politicians known as the Santa Fe Ring had over New Mexico.[12]

It was about this same time that Tolby had an altercation with Judge Joseph Palen on the streets of Cimarron. The disagreement was probably related to the lack of charges against Pancho Griego. Frank Springer testified to the encounter: "During the first week in September 1875, while the court was in session at Cimarron, Judge Palen and Tolby had a rather spirited altercation, the judge denouncing him for some remarks he had made about the court and its actions. Tolby immediately declared he would 'write up that judge so that 200,000 readers should see his record.'" The comment by Tolby led to speculation that he was the author of the July letter in the *New York Sun* that was critical of Palen and the Santa Fe Ring. Whether Tolby actually wrote the letter is still a matter of debate, though the *New York Sun* later reported that Tolby "never wrote a line for" the paper.[13]

On Thursday, September 9, mail contractor Florencio Donoghue, a man said to be connected to the Santa Fe Ring, accosted Tolby on the streets of Cimarron. F. J. Tolby was in front of the St. James Hotel barroom having a conversation with James Coleman when a very drunk Donoghue approached Tolby, cursing out the reverend and looking for a fight. As James Gilchrist intervened and took hold of Donoghue, Donoghue threatened Tolby, saying, "I will kill you, you son of a bitch."[14]

The line between the two sides in Colfax County were clearly drawn. On one side was a tightknit group of men in power—referred to by detractors as the Santa Fe Ring—and on the other were citizens of Colfax County and surrounding areas who were challenging their power and working to put a spotlight on what they saw as the underhanded scheming of the Ring to gain power, land, and wealth at the expense of the citizens of New Mexico. Up to this time the conflict had been mostly peaceful as each side attempted to fight in the courts, the press, and the ballot box, but that was about to change. The clouds gathered, the sky darkened, and the storm was about to begin.

Chapter 4

Violence in Colfax County

On Sunday, September 12, F. J. Tolby was scheduled to hold services in Elizabethtown but did not make it in time. He arrived later that evening, citing the condition of his horse as the cause of his delay.[1]

On Tuesday, September 14, Tolby left E-town, located in the hills looking down on the Moreno Valley, and passed through the valley. He stopped at the home of Henry Pascoe for fifteen to twenty minutes, then left Pascoe's and entered the wooded mountains on the road through Cimarron Canyon that led to Cimarron. He did not reach home.

Back in Cimarron, Mary Tolby was at home with the couple's two children (some reports say she was pregnant with a third child, who would be named Frank, but no further record of him has been found. If there was a Frank, he likely died young). There may also have been an unidentified "wounded man" still staying at the house, whom the Tolbys had been watching over shortly before Tolby left. Mary expected her husband to return Wednesday or Thursday. As Thursday passed she became concerned. It was that evening that the horrible news came. A man identified only as Taylor found the body of Frank Tolby lying in the brush off the road cutting through Cimarron Canyon. He had been shot. Later examination showed two bullets entered his body from behind, with at least one of the bullets entering near the heart. Tolby's body

37

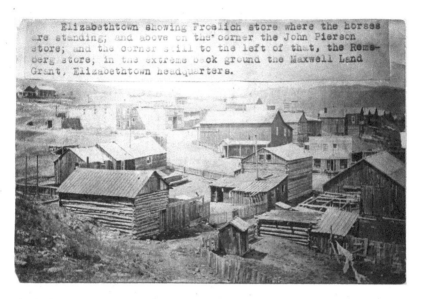

Elizabethtown, circa 1890. Photographer unknown. Negative #014635, Palace of the Governors Photo Archives, Santa Fe, NM (NMHM/DCA).

was found near a point where two roads—the road Tolby was traveling and the "old road"—met to cross a bridge. It was believed that Tolby was killed at the bridge. Tolby's horse was found tied to a tree and none of his belongings were missing, so robbery was ruled out as a motive. No other evidence was found as the tracks of the killers were destroyed by rain.[2]

Tolby's body was brought to Cimarron, where it was examined by a coroner's jury. Franklin J. Tolby was buried with Masonic honors on Saturday, September 18, 1875. He was dead at 33, leaving behind his wife, Mary, and their children, Rachel and Grace (and possibly the yet-to-be-born Frank). His widow and their children and went to her parents' home in Indiana.[3]

It was learned that Constable Cruz Vega, who was also working as a temporary mail carrier for one day—the day Tolby was killed—entered Cimarron Canyon shortly after Tolby, and it was believed by some that if he wasn't involved in the assassination, he must have seen or heard something. Sixty-two or sixty-three-year-old Samuel H. Irwin, who was part of the coroner's jury, visited the murder scene.[4] He later testified that he measured

Road through Cimarron Canyon between Cimarron and Elizabethtown, circa 1872–80. Photograph by Byron H. Gurnsey. Author's collection.

the main road (the one that Tolby took) and the old road (the road said to have been taken by Vega) and found that the old road was about 660 yards shorter from where the roads split to their intersection at the bridge where Tolby was murdered. Irwin stated that Andrew Howell told him "that Tolby was not more than one half mile ahead of Vega at the time he entered the

Moreno Valley, February 1943. Photograph by John Collier Jr. Reproduction Number LC-DIG-fsac-1a34506, Library of Congress Prints and Photographs Division, Library of Congress, Washington, DC.

canyon near Pascoe's ranch. . . . Tolby got to Pascoe's first and stopped some 15 or 20 minutes. A few minutes after, Vega came along and got some letters. Pascoe's is six miles from Elizabethtown. . . . Tolbys [*sic*] horse was poor and slow. The mail carrier was a fast rider." According to Irwin, Howell questioned Vega about Tolby's murder but "could not get anything from him, and he was contradictory in his statements."[5]

The Free Masons offered a $500 reward for the apprehension of Tolby's killers. Governor Samuel B. Axtell followed this by offering a $500 reward on behalf of the territory for the apprehension and conviction of the guilty person or persons.[6] Despite this, there didn't appear to be much action taken by the territory or local law enforcement to find the assassins.

Feeling that local authorities were not doing enough to catch Tolby's killer, his former assistant, Oscar P. McMains, took it upon himself to

Mary Tolby. This photo of Mary was taken many years after the death of Franklin. She had remarried and was now Mary Smith. The year and photographer are unknown. James Klaiber Collection, Lafayette, IN.

investigate the murder. The 34 or 35 years old McMains was born and raised in Milford, Ohio, a suburb of Cincinnati, in 1840. Life changed for Oscar and his four siblings when their mother, Nancy, died in the early 1850s. Shortly after, his grief-stricken father, Robert, left with one of his sons for California. The youngest daughter was adopted by another family while Oscar, along with sister Mary Louise and brother Billy, were either on their own or cared for by their mother's sister, Debbie Mount.

At about 15 years of age, Oscar learned to be a printer. He was around 18 when he joined the Methodist Episcopal Church and began preaching a year later when the church appointed him, on trial, to Beverly, Illinois. He spent a few years preaching in several Illinois communities and became an ordained deacon. In 1864 he was made an elder, declined another appointment in Illinois, and headed west to the territory of Colorado.

At the annual Colorado Conference of the Methodist Episcopal Church in 1864, McMains was assigned to Black Hawk, Colorado (although he wasn't present for the conference, arriving after it had adjourned). Over the next few years, McMains served in Burlington, Loveland, Central, Nevadaville, and Pueblo. McMains also had some of his poetry published in the *Daily Rocky Mountain News*, wrote articles and poetry for the *Colorado Daily Chieftain* under the pseudonym "A. Bach," and showed a gift for public speaking.

The young man had personal troubles when a young woman he was taken with, Luna Jordan, became interested in another man. Because of this, at the 1870 Colorado Conference of the Methodist Episcopal Church when it was announced that McMains would return to Pueblo, the jilted lover sprang to his feet and declared that he would not go back. However, he soon agreed to accept the assignment. During the 1871 Colorado Conference, McMains was "granted a location at his own request" and he became a traveling elder (a minister not limited to a single location). Whether this was due to the personal reasons that made him want to leave Pueblo a year earlier is not known. While McMains served the church as a traveling elder, other problems that had surfaced over the past year became more pronounced. McMains became vocal about some of his liberal attitudes that went against church positions, the key one being that he had no objection to dancing (which was banned by the church). This rift grew larger with time. J. H. Merrit, who took over Pueblo, challenged McMains on the dancing issue, insisting that dancing in any form was sinful.[7]

On April 19, 1872, McMains resigned from the church but asked to keep the parchments that certified his ministerial status. This request was granted. He did this because he had no intention of giving up preaching. He continued on his own and was given the use of a schoolhouse in Pueblo to hold services. McMains spent the next couple of years preaching, writing, and engaged in public speaking. But Methodism was a part of him and eventually he returned, and was accepted, back into the Methodist Episcopal Church as a traveling elder. In October of 1874, McMains was transferred by the church to Saguache, but this didn't last long because in 1875 he moved to the territory of New Mexico.[8]

Oscar P. McMains. Date and photographer unknown. Western History
Department, Denver Public Library, Denver, CO.

O. P. McMains settled in Cimarron, where he became Tolby's assistant.
He took a job as a printer for the *Cimarron News and Press* and quickly
became part of the community, even reading an original, patriotic poem in a
Cimarron Fourth of July event. Despite becoming involved in the community
so quickly, he was prepared for a short stay. As summer came to a close,

McMains received an appointment to go to Silver City. However, after the murder of Franklin Tolby, he decided to stay in Cimarron. McMains was appointed to ride Tolby's former circuit. While doing so he investigated his friend's murder.[9]

Another of Tolby's colleagues who undertook to investigate the murder was New Mexico Missions superintendent Thomas Harwood. Reverend Harwood was in Chicago when he learned of Tolby's death. Upon hearing the news, he hurried back to New Mexico. Shortly after arriving in the territory, Harwood heard that a man (Manuel Cardenas) who had returned to Taos from Elizabethtown had said "that a Protestant heretic had been killed." Harwood remembered that he said this "before it was known in his own neighborhood," which led Harwood to believe that he knew something about the murder, so Harwood and a preacher named Roberts went to Taos to find this man. They failed in the search and soon concluded that it was best to stay out of the investigation and not contribute to an unstable situation. Harwood and McMains clashed over this, as McMains was determined to find Tolby's assassins and whoever had planned the murder. Harwood recalled,

> I would not be led by him and he would not be advised by me. And because I would not be led by him he construed it to mean that I was against him and against the efforts to ferret out the mysterious murder of Mr. Tolby. . . . My advice was for us to go right on in our missionary work as if nothing had occurred, but at the same time keep our eyes and ears open for all we could see and hear and as 'murder will out,' I thought we would be more apt to get on the track of the murderers in that way than in any other. Mr. McMains's plan was to quit everything else and hunt down the assassins.[10]

Follow his own plan McMains did. Joining McMains in his hunt for Tolby's killer or killers was rancher Clay Allison.

Robert A. Clay Allison was born on the second day of September 1841 in Wayne County, Tennessee. He was the fourth of nine children (although one had died before Clay's birth). Nothing is known of Clay's youth. His next appearance in the historical record is his enlistment in the Confederate Army on October 15, 1861. Clay, with his brothers Jesse and Jeremiah, joined a light

Thomas Harwood. Date and photographer unknown. ID #WVM.1549.I001, Wisconsin Veterans Museum, Madison, WI.

artillery company under Captain J. Wesley Eldridge.[11] Allison's first military stint did not last long. He was discharged in January 1862 because he was judged to be "unfit for duty." The doctor who examined him reported, "I certify that I have carefully examined the said R. A. C. Allison of Cap't Eldridge's Artillery Company, and find him incapable of performing the duties of a soldier—because of a blow received many years ago, producing no doubt a depression of the Scull [sic], Since which time, febrile, emotional or physical excitement produces paroxysmal [a sudden attack or outburst] of a mixed

Robert "Clay" Allison, circa 1865. Photographer unknown. Reprint from *Clay Allison: Portrait of a Shootist* by Chuck Parsons. Permission to publish courtesy of West of the Pecos Museum, Pecos, TX.

character, partly Epileptic & partly Maniacal. He is now suffering from such a paroxysm, caused by an attack of Pneumonia during which he manifests a great disposition to Commit Suicide." The discharge papers describe Allison as "5 feet 9 inches high, light complexion, blue eyes, dark hair, and by occupation when enlisted a farmer."[12] Allison reenlisted in September 1862 at Leatherwood, Tennessee, in Company F of the 19th Tennessee Cavalry under Colonel Jacob B. Biffle. Allison fought for the Confederacy until the war's end.[13]

After the war, Allison became involved in the Wayne County Ku Klux Klan and at some point soon after (if not right from the beginning) would serve the organization as the Grand Cyclops, making him leader of the Wayne County KKK. Started as mainly a social club after the war, the KKK soon morphed into a political organization that more and more relied on intimidation, violence, and domestic terrorism to keep Republicans from the polls and limit the rights of the newly freed Blacks. In August 1868 Allison pledged to have the men under him stop all raiding and violence, and soon after he cut ties with the organization as he left Tennessee for Texas.[14]

Clay Allison eventually moved farther west to New Mexico, where he became a rancher. Clay, with his younger brother John, established a ranch on the Vermejo River, north of Cimarron. Allison had "a full black beard" around this time and walked with a limp because of a self-inflicted gunshot wound. During these postwar years it's been said he was involved in a few killings and the lynching of Elizabethtown serial killer Charles Kennedy, who murdered guests at his roadside inn, but the only one that can be definitely attributed to Allison is his January 1874 shooting of Chunk Colbert. Colbert, a rancher in Colfax County, was wanted for the cold-blooded murder of George Waller the previous December. After already avoiding arrest at least once, Colbert inexplicably returned to the area, where he spent a day drinking and becoming increasingly angry and belligerent. His firearm received much use that day as he shot up a saloon and shot a man named Charles Cooper in the hand while trying to kill someone else. One of the men Colbert quarreled with was Clay Allison. Later the same day, Colbert and Allison shared a table at Clifton House, a stage stop where they went for a meal. Allison kept close watch on Colbert, and when Colbert raised his gun and took a shot at Allison, Clay dove out of the way, quickly drew his gun, and shot Colbert just above the right eye. There were no immediate charges against Allison as it was clearly a case of self-defense.[15]

Clay Allison was described by people in Cimarron as well-mannered and likeable, and as having a "flair for humor" when sober, but as troublesome and someone "to be avoided" when drunk. It was as a rancher in Colfax County that he came to know and admire Reverend F. J. Tolby, even though Tolby was staunchly against the Santa Fe Ring and Allison had supported the Ring's candidates, including congressman Elkins and other local officials. Tolby's assassination, however, changed Allison's views.[16]

Oscar McMains, Clay Allison, and others soon became convinced that Cruz Vega was involved in the murder of Tolby. Vega had been hired by Florencio Donoghue to carry the mail from Elizabethtown to

Cimarron on the day of Tolby's murder and for that day only. Furthermore, a witness, Andrew J. Howell, said Vega entered Cimarron Canyon shortly after Tolby.[17]

McMains and other citizens decided that Vega needed to be questioned. The general feeling in town was that local law enforcement—under Sheriff Orson K. Chittenden—was not interested in tracking down Tolby's assassin. Existing evidence suggests not much had been done to solve the mystery. Reasons for this are unknown. Chittenden was no friend of the Santa Fe Ring, so protecting them wasn't likely a motivating factor for the sheriff. It's possible he was working quietly out of public view on the case, but no records of what Chittenden had done exist and no arrests had been made. Because of the perceived inaction, McMains put together a plan to question Vega. He first tried to enlist Isaiah Rinehart to help him get Vega out to a secluded spot on the Ponil River to question him, but Rinehart refused to get involved, so McMains approached William Low to ask for his assistance to get Vega alone. Low, attracted by the reward, agreed to help. Low owned a cornfield by Ponil River and the plan was for him to hire Vega to guard the corn from wild animals.[18]

William Low hired Cruz Vega for three nights. On the second night, a cold Saturday, October 30, Low went out with Vega. They built a fire and after a while the two men fell asleep. They were awakened by a group of about four to six men, suspected to have been led by Clay Allison. While Low and Vega stood up, one of the men said, "Hello, boys" as he walked up to them and threw a rope around Vega's neck. "Come on," he said as he pulled the rope to take Vega with them. Taking Low as well, the men walked to a telegraph line, where forty to fifty men were waiting. It was dark except for a small fire. Low was told he could go, but he stayed nearby in the crowd while the men who had Vega took him to a telegraph pole. Oscar McMains stood away from the pole and called out questions for them to ask Cruz Vega. At one point one of the men with Vega climbed the telegraph pole and threw the other end of the rope around Vega's neck over the telegraph line. The men pulled Cruz Vega up the pole by his neck, held him for a few seconds, then released him. McMains again called out questions to ask him. The desperate Vega told the crowd that yes, he was present when F. J. Tolby was murdered, but it wasn't he who killed the reverend; it was Manuel Cardenas. Vega claimed two other men, Florencio Donoghue and his uncle, Pancho Griego, planned the murder.[19]

McMains had some conversation with all of the party except those holding Vega. The men, satisfied with Vega's statement, left Vega with the small group who had already pulled him up the telegraph pole. McMains later claimed the men were too drunk on whiskey to control, but it doesn't appear that McMains tried very hard, if at all, to convince them to release Vega before he withdrew. McMains crossed a bridge over the Ponil River and returned to Simeon Erastus Welding's house, where he was boarding. William Low, who was also staying at Welding's house, for some reason waded through the river instead of using the bridge and arrived at Welding's shortly after McMains. Oscar McMains was in bed when he heard shots fired. According to Welding, McMains exclaimed, "I fear those are the shots that killed Cruz Vega." McMains was correct, he had just heard the murder of Vega.[20]

Chapter 5

Gunfight at the St. James Hotel and Arrests Made

Two days after the Cruz Vega lynching, on Monday, November 1, 1875, Clay Allison and some friends went to the barroom of the St. James Hotel, which stood across the street from the Maxwell Land Grant and Railway Company headquarters. The barroom, with its monte, poker, billiard, and roulette tables (one of each), was the most popular saloon in town. An angry Pancho Griego, who was Cruz Vega's uncle, met Allison at the door of the saloon and accused Allison of being one of the vigilantes who murdered Vega. They kept their emotions under control long enough to agree to go inside for a drink. The two men walked to the corner of the barroom. After a brief time talking, the furious Griego went for his gun, but Allison saw the movement, beat him to the draw, and quickly fired three shots into his enemy. With Griego's corpse lying on the wooden floor in a pool of blood, Henry Lambert made everyone leave and closed up for the night. Griego's body stayed where he fell until the following morning.[1] The *Santa Fe New Mexican* reported, "Griego was well known in Santa Fe where his mother resides. He has killed a great many men, and was considered as a dangerous man; few regret his loss."[2]

St. James Hotel, center, circa 1877. Photographer unknown. Old Aztec Mill
Museum, Cimarron, NM.

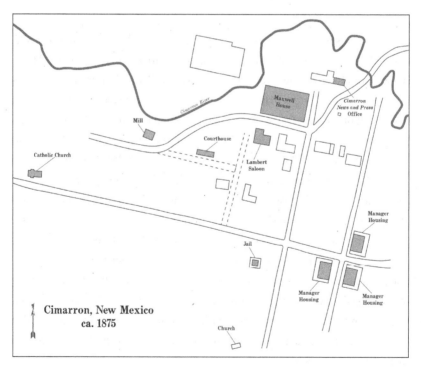

Map of Cimarron in 1875. Map by Lori Goodloe.

Juan Francisco "Pancho" Griego. Date and photographer unknown. Western History Department, Denver Public Library, Denver, CO.

Following the Griego killing, Clay Allison and friends engaged in an alcohol-fueled spree. Ada Morley, who was staying at the ranch of Manley and Theresa Chase while her husband was in Las Vegas on business, visited Cimarron to get the latest news and made notes about the happenings in town. She wrote that on Tuesday, November 2, the day after he killed Griego, "Allison and 12 friends charged into Cimarron [at] 11 o'clock terrifying everybody." After a quiet Wednesday, the binge picked up on Thursday. Morley wrote, *"Thursday, Nov. 4th*. Allison and a great many friends came in at three. Dawson, Clutton, Cook all mistreated, left at dark." The drunken misbehavior continued the next evening. Of Friday Morley recorded: "Quiet in the day. At dark Allison (with four friends) rode into Lambert's . . . had war dance over Pancho's blood. Music."[3] Another account of the war dance had it culminating with "Allison stripping naked & dancing around with a ribbon tied to his penis."[4]

Robert "Clay" Allison, circa 1868. Photographer unknown. West of the Pecos
Museum, Pecos, TX.

Cimarron, circa 1877. Photographer unknown. Resource Identifier 000-742-0627, William A. Keleher Collection, Center for Southwest Research, University of New Mexico.

The day of Allison's war dance, action was finally taken to depose the man implicated by Cruz Vega in the murder of Reverend Tolby. Manuel Cardenas, about 40 years old, was arrested in Taos and taken to Elizabethtown, where he was examined by Justice of the Peace Dallas Cummings. Under oath Cardenas claimed Pancho Griego told him that Cruz Vega assassinated Franklin Tolby. What he added to the story was more important than who pulled the trigger. Cardenas claimed that Vega was hired to kill Tolby by Judge Robert H. Longwill, attorney Melvin Mills, mail carrier Florencio Donoghue, and Francisco Griego, all of whom were closely connected to the Santa Fe Ring.[5] Cardenas stated, "I had some conversation with Dr. Longwill at his office. He said to me that he, Donoghue, Mills, and Griego paid Cruz Vega the sum of five hundred dollars to kill Tolby. Longwill offered me the same amount to kill F. J. Tolby. I told him I would not do it for any consideration. This offer was made me on the 12th or 13th of September. Donoghue was the Treasurer of the combination of persons above stated who contrived and planned the killing of F. J. Tolby. Longwill told me that Donoghue was the man that had the money."

Cummings asked him, "Why did Longwill tell you that Donoghue had five hundred dollars to pay Cruz Vega?"

"Because he wanted me to do the work."

"What was it you wanted to tell private to us?"

"First, Dr. Longwill called me into his office and offered me five hundred dollars to kill Tolby," Cardenas said. "I told him I would not do it. Longwill said it did not make any difference, for he had men that would do it, men paid to do it."

"Did Pancho [Griego] tell you anything about this affair?"

"He did. He told me they had paid money to the mail carrier to kill Tolby."

Cummings asked, "Why did Pancho tell you this?"

"Because he was a friend of mine. He said this is private, between you and me. He then said, we have got a man hired to kill Tolby. He said they had given the money to Donoghue to give to Cruz Vega. Longwill told me that the money was for Cruz Vega. He told me the 12th or 13th of September when I was in his office. He wanted me to kill him. I would not do it. He then told me he had Cruz Vega hired. Pancho told me that Donoghue had the five hundred dollars for Vega on the 13th or 14th. Pancho told me on Tuesday night that Tolby had been killed. He told me I was a damned fool, that I might have had five hundred dollars in my pocket as well as not. He said if you betray me or the other men we will kill you."

"Where were you on Monday?"

"I was in Cimarron and went to the mill, bought a sack of flour from Bob Allen, then went to my mother-in-law's house. Tuesday morning I went to Tison's house and took two bundles of clothes to Francisca Costa, Tison's woman. Tison was present. Then I went home to work. I worked at home until I started to Taos, which was, I think, on Friday September 17th or 18th." His statement complete, the illiterate Cardenas signed it with an "X."[6]

Cardenas's statement included some significant names. The accusation that Longwill and Mills, along with Donoghue and Griego (whom Vega had implicated), were behind the murder is important not only because of Mills and Longwill's connection to the Santa Fe Ring but also because of their positions of power. Years later Thomas Harwood wrote that Tolby told him about the fight he witnessed where Francisco Griego murdered two soldiers and said Tolby declared his intention to testify before the grand jury. Harwood opined that Griego, whom Tolby was determined to testify against, was behind Tolby's murder. Many years after, in defense of himself, Melvin Mills gave the opinion that Tolby was killed because "he openly declared that he saw Donoghue and Griego shoot at some Americans and that he intended to go before the Grand Jury and secure and [*sic*] indictment."[7]

Donoghue was not involved in the shooting, but it's possible Donoghue was helping his friend Griego after the incident. If the plot to kill Tolby began with Griego and Donoghue, and was to protect Griego from prosecution, why bring in Mills and Longwill? If the statement of Cardenas is accurate, were Mills and Longwill just helping a friend, or did they want Tolby eliminated for other reasons? Frank Springer later stated that a man named Lara told him that Griego was promised that he wouldn't face consequences for his actions if he would use his influence among the native New Mexicans in favor of Elkins and Longwill in the coming election.[8] Was a deal struck to help Griego? Maybe, but the problem with connecting Tolby's assassination to this deal is that the district court session had happened before Tolby's murder and the grand jury had already decided not to indict Griego. Another possibility is that Tolby was assassinated to silence him. Not only was he outspoken against the Santa Fe Ring, but his altercation with Judge Palen, which made some believe Tolby was the author of the first letter published in the *New York Sun* that was critical of New Mexico politicians and the Ring, happened just a week before his death. William Morley claimed, in an unrelated affidavit, that Longwill once told him "that the right way to run a country was to get somebody to shoot the sons-of-bitches who opposed you."[9] Many in Cimarron were convinced this was the reason for Tolby's assassination.

Cardenas's statement led to Justice of the Peace Samuel S. Trauer issuing warrants for the arrest of Longwill, Mills, and Donoghue. Longwill heard of the confession and left town that night, worried that he would suffer the same fate as Cruz Vega if he stayed. Early on the morning of Sunday, November 7, 1875, Donoghue and Mills were taken into custody. That same morning Deputy Pete Burleson, with Clay and John Allison, went in pursuit of Longwill, who went to Fort Union, where he was hidden from his pursuers by officers. After his pursuers headed back to Cimarron, Longwill went to Santa Fe.[10]

Robert H. Longwill. Donald S. Dreesen Collection of Pictures of Prominent New Mexicans, Center for Southwest Research, University of New Mexico, Albuquerque, NM.

Cimarron's reputation for violence was growing as reports spread that the town was in a state of anarchy. At the request of Governor Axtell, soldiers arrived in town on Monday, November 8, to restore order. Many in Cimarron saw this step as unnecessary and as simply a way for the Santa Fe Ring to cast those outraged over Tolby's assassination as a mob. The same day that the soldiers arrived, Manuel Cardenas retracted his confession, claiming it was forced out of him. On top of all this, Santa Fe Ring–connected attorney Henry Waldo was able to get writs of habeas corpus to have defendants Donoghue, Longwill, and Mills transferred to Santa Fe County, though he

Colfax County Courthouse, Cimarron, August 1936. Photo by Frederick D. Nichols. Call Number HABS NM, 4-CIM,4-2, Library of Congress Prints and Photographs Division, Library of Congress, Washington, DC.

ended up backing down from this and let their cases be heard in Cimarron. While all this was going on, the interested and curious from around the county flooded into Cimarron.[11]

On the morning of Wednesday, November 10, Robert Clay Allison appeared before Justice of the Peace Samuel Trauer at Cimarron for killing Griego. Justice of the Peace Dallas Cummings of Elizabethtown sat with Trauer, whose job it was to determine if there was enough evidence to refer the case to the grand jury. Allison admitted to the killing, and while the prosecution didn't call any witnesses, the defense called several. According to the *Cimarron News and Press*, "It was clearly proven that Allison had been threatened and his life was in danger from Griego." The killing was ruled to be justifiable homicide and Clay Allison was released.[12]

That afternoon, Justices Trauer and Cummings heard the cases against Melvin Mills, Florencio Donoghue, and Manuel Cardenas. Mills hired Frank Springer to represent him, while Oscar P. McMains called and examined witnesses for the territory. Why McMains, who had no legal background, was chosen for this task is not known.[13]

The first witness called was Samuel Irwin. He stated, "I was present at the Coroner's inquest on the remains of Rev. Tolby. . . . The coroner's jury and those present at the inquest differed as to whether the shots were fired by one or two persons." Irwin said that some thought one person could not have fired both shots. He described the murder scene and gave evidence implicating Cruz Vega. Several other witnesses testified to Tolby's movements the day of the murder and Vega's statement the night of his lynching. Then the topic switched to the since-retracted statement of Manuel Cardenas, which O. P. McMains read to the court. Following the reading, multiple people who witnessed Cardenas giving the statement testified that he was not coerced into giving it.[14]

Shifting from Cardenas to Donoghue, James Coleman and James Gilchrist both testified to Florencio Donoghue's confrontation with Franklin Tolby the week before Tolby's murder, when Donoghue approached Tolby in front of the St. James Hotel and accosted the reverend, seemingly looking for a fight. According to Gilchrist, after he had hold of Donoghue to keep him back, Donoghue threatened Tolby, telling him, "I will kill you, you son of a bitch." Following this, multiple witnesses, including Clay Allison, were allowed to give hearsay evidence that others told them they heard Donoghue threaten to kill Tolby, and other witnesses said they heard Donoghue make similar threats about McMains since Tolby's assassination.[15]

Irvin W. Lacy testified that after Vega was killed but before Cardenas's statement, he had a conversation with Longwill about the investigation into Tolby's murder in which Longwill expressed the hope that the investigation would stop.[16]

The hearing then moved to the case against Melvin Mills. Clay Allison retook the stand and was asked about a conversation he had with Mills the previous day. Mills had expressed concern that circumstantial evidence was against him. Allision testified, "He said that in many things he had been led and influenced by Dr. Longwill, and blinded by him."[17] Nothing of substance was presented against Mills.

With the final set of witnesses, attention turned back to Manuel Cardenas. Jules Howard testified, "Cardenas's reputation in Taos is bad . . . his reputation was that of a murderer and thief." Turning to the killing of Tolby, Howard stated, "I heard in Taos that Cardenas had brought the word there of Tolby's death."[18]

Further testimony about the reputation of Cardenas was followed by the much more important issue of his alibi. In his statement at Elizabethtown, Cardenas had said that on the morning of Tolby's murder he was in Cimarron and had visited the home of a man name Tison. That same man, identified only as Mr. Tison, took the stand. He stated unequivocally, "Cardenas was not at my house on Tuesday morning, the day of Tolby's murder."[19] Following this was more testimony about Cardenas, his reputation, his statement, and its retraction.

Next, Melvin Mills made a statement in his own defense. Mills declared his innocence and said he came to Cimarron voluntarily to have his day in court after hearing of the charges against him. Of his relationship with Longwill, Mills testified that he hadn't been on friendly terms with him until the past year, and stated, "I always distrusted his friendship."[20]

Florencio Donoghue spoke next. He acknowledged he had arguments with Tolby but said he never wanted to hurt him. Of the threats he made against Tolby, Donoghue stated he had no memory of what he said when drunk, and added that he had been "under the influence of liquor" for the past two months.[21] At this point a recess was taken.

Following the recess, Justices of the Peace Trauer and Cummings found convincing evidence against Cardenas and ordered that he be held in jail until the grand jury could hear his case. Donoghue was also ordered back to jail to await action of the grand jury, with bail set at $20,000. They released Mills for lack of evidence and made no ruling in Longwill's case since he was not in custody.[22]

It was late when court adjourned after a long day of testimony. Under the night sky, two guards escorted Cardenas back to jail. Near their destination, a group of as many as twenty unknown men rushed out from behind the jail and were said to have "overpowered" the guards. One of the group fired a single gunshot into the head of Manuel Cardenas and the men quickly fled under the cover of the night. Cardenas died instantly. Troops rushed to the scene after hearing the gunfire, but the killers were gone by the time they arrived.[23]

Cimarron Jail years after the Colfax County War. The crumbling outer wall was intact in the 1870s. Photographer unknown. Courtesy of Len Gratteri.

Whoever killed Manuel Cardenas was never identified. Some have said, though not until many years later, that Clay Allison led the mob and fired the shot. It is possible some of the men were the same group who lynched Cruz Vega. However, if this was the case, it was a crucial mistake, as a dead Cardenas couldn't give more information as to why Tolby was assassinated. Others believe that whoever killed Cardenas did so to keep him from telling what he knew. While this is logical, if politicians connected with the Santa Fe Ring were behind Cardenas's killing, it is unlikely they would have employed so many men to carry out the job, as it would increase the possibility of someone from this group confessing later.[24]

That evening, concerned citizens of Colfax County gathered at the courthouse in Cimarron to discuss the recent violence. O. P. McMains was elected chairman of the meeting. Clay Allison was nominated to be one of four vice presidents but asked that his name be withdrawn from consideration. Frank Springer, acting as secretary, recorded a list of resolutions said to have been agreed upon by all who attended. At the meeting's conclusion, Springer read the resolutions. After a general introduction, Springer read to the group, "On the 14th day of September, A. D. 1875, the Rev. F. J. Tolby, a minister of the gospel resident among us, and a man who for sterling qualities, both as a minster and a citizen, commanded the highest respect and esteem among all the people of this county, was foully assassinated, while traveling upon the public highway, and, whereas, the report of this murder, circulated abroad, has created an impression, that the lives of peaceable citizens are not safe here, and has thereby worked a great detriment and injury to our county. . . ." It was agreed that, "for the sake of justice and the good name and reputation of our community," there must be prompt punishment of those guilty of the heinous crime. The resolution continued,

> efforts have been made by various of our citizens, which have led to the capture of certain parties, and an accumulation of evidence which leaves no room for doubt that the real murderers have been discovered.
>
> That the facts disclosed reveal deliberately planned assassination, in which the men Cruz Vega and Manuel Cardinas [sic] were the tools of other parties, who from some motive, aside from plunder, planned the murder and procured the two men above named to perform the cowardly act.
>
> That we regard those who procured the commission of the murder as far more guilty, if possible, than the duped and hired tools, and that if satisfactory evidence is found to discover and identify any such party or parties there should not be permitted to them any loophole to escape the extreme penalty of the law.
>
> We are not a mob of lawless men, as has been reported abroad, bent upon violence and defiance of law, but on the contrary, have assembled legally and quietly for the purpose of securing the doing of justice and the punishment of crime.

The resolution further stated that they would punish no one on "insufficient or doubtful evidence."[25]

The resolution condemned the United States Army at Fort Union for hiding Robert Longwill and protecting him from arrest. About the troops that Axtell thought necessary to send to Cimarron, Springer read from the resolution "that our thanks are due to Lieutenant Cornish for the fair, proper, and dignified manner in which he has performed his duties while here, and that while we consider the sending of troops here as uncalled for and unnecessary, the courteous and forbearing manner in which the power has been used by the Lieutenant's Command has avoided all collision and difficulty."[26]

The *Cimarron News and Press* reported that on the morning following the meeting "most of the people from other parts of the county departed for their homes, the large crowd quietly dispersed and the town renewed its wonted quiet appearance." The commentary continued,

> Thus ended what was probably the most remarkable movement ever witnessed in Colfax County. For four days the town was filled with a constantly increasing crowd of people from every part of the county who were laboring under a feeling of intense and earnest excitement. The whole county seemed to be aroused and animated by a common sentiment. Men left their homes and their business, and gave up everything in order to attend and participate in the proceedings. These seemed to be but a single feeling and that was an unbending determination to bring to light the facts of this murderous assassination and to insure the punishment of the guilty parties. . . . The proceedings without exception (save the one act of unknown persons in killing Cardinas [*sic*]) were determined and earnest, while they were sober and dignified.

While it may have been true that the crowds in Cimarron were peaceful (and there is no indication they were not), the murder of a prisoner in the custody of law enforcement, with little to no effort made to find the persons responsible, undercuts any claim that law and order was prevailing. The *News and Press* report continued, "Continual surprise was manifested by persons coming from the south, at the condition of peace and order which they found. It had been reported that our town was in a state of riot and confusion, that a reign of terror existed, and it was not safe to pass through here, so that when people came to see the true state of affairs, they would scarcely believe their eyes." As to the soldiers in Cimarron, the commentary read, "Lieutenant Cornish and a detachment which had been ordered here . . . found nothing to do.

The soldiers mingled freely with the citizens, and were interested spectators of all the proceedings."[27]

From the outside, however, Cimarron's reputation of violence continued. The *Gazette* from nearby Las Vegas, New Mexico, commented, "Cimarron is becoming a decidedly interesting neighborhood and Life Insurance Companies are instructing agents not to take any more risks in that section," while the *Western Christian Advocate*, a Methodist newspaper in Cincinnati that had been reporting on Tolby's assassination and subsequent events, editorialized, "Whether Cimarron is a more desirable place for a preacher of the Gospel than among the cannibals, who are said to love missionary soup, is a question. . . ."[28] Citizens of Cimarron had work to do to rehabilitate the town's reputation.

Chapter 6

Bill Signed

Judge Joseph Palen, chief justice of the New Mexico Supreme Court, died of natural causes in his Santa Fe home on December 21, 1875. The loss of a Ring influence controlling the court wouldn't last long. Although his replacement as chief justice, Henry Waldo, was a Democrat, he was also a boyhood friend of Stephen Elkins, had strong ties to the Santa Fe Ring, and sided with the Ring on issues of mutual interest.[1]

Shortly before Palen's death, on December 16, another letter, said to have come from Santa Fe, appeared in the *New York Sun*. Under the headline "Territory of Elkins," the letter opened, "The political revolution which has taken place and is still in progress in this Territory is mainly attributed to the exposures of the Santa Fé Ring which have appeared in THE SUN, and which have created great consternation among our corrupt officials, THE SUN having a very wide circulation in this region." The writer accurately summed up the events connected with the murder of F. J. Tolby and followed this with speculation about the Santa Fe Ring's involvement in the killing. Stating that Tolby had threatened to expose the Ring in the press, and that some believed he had written a letter that had been published in the *Sun*, many thought the Santa Fe Ring was behind the assassination. The peoples' anger grew when Vega and Cardenas "implicated the principal members of the Colfax county branch of the Ring as the instigators of the crime." The correspondent further stated, "Although there is no legal evidence to prove that the recognized leaders of the Ring either had any connection with the assassination of Mr. Tolby, or knew that such an atrocious crime was in contemplation; yet it is impossible to make the majority of the people in Cimarron and vicinity believe that they are altogether guiltless, and the feeling against all persons who are supposed to be connected in any way with the operations of Elkins & Co. is bitter in the extreme."[2]

In the December 31 issue of the *Cimarron News and Press*, editor Will Dawson surprised many in Colfax County by denouncing the letter in the *Sun*, calling it "another one of those lying, brutal letters." In a scathing editorial, Dawson opined, "The writer, whoever he may be, will be looked upon as a coward, a disturber of the peace, as well as a slanderer upon the good name and fair fame of this portion of New Mexico." He condemned the writer for "keeping alive the bad condition of feeling in this country" and for going to a paper outside of the territory with "villainous tirades" against New Mexico citizens.[3] Dawson also attacked *New York Sun* editor Charles Anderson Dana for printing the letter.[4]

Angry Colfax citizens sent a letter to Dawson and the *News and Press*, declaring that the accusations made in the letter to the *Sun* were true, and that Dawson's condemnation of it was "unjust in the extreme." The message to Dawson contended that the recent letter, as well as the letters published in the *Sun* earlier in the year, "have opened the eyes of the world to the corruptions which have and do exist in New Mexican politics, and we hope and trust the *Sun* and the newspaper press generally will continue their efforts until a thorough investigation, from proper sources, is made which will bring about a better state of things." The citizens writing to Dawson further opined that "the action of the people in investigating the Tolby murderers and punishing such of them as were caught, was a public necessity, and for the public good, inasmuch as the history of the past few years has shown that through the regular legal actions of the authorities in power, such cruel and bloodthirsty deeds are not likely to be punished." One hundred and fifty-three citizens of Colfax County signed the letter, including Samuel Irwin, Clay Allison, O. P. McMains, and Dawson's coeditors at the *News and Press*, William Morley and Frank Springer.[5] On January 7 Springer and Morley resigned from the paper because they did not agree with Dawson's editorial policy.[6] They released the following statement in the *News and Press*: "On account of disagreement as to the management, political and otherwise, of the NEWS AND PRESS, the undersigned withdraw from editorial connection with the paper until negotiations now pending can be settled as to the future course of the paper, and we disclaim any responsibility for the issue of last week save two brief items . . . which were written some weeks ago."[7]

On December 6, 1875, Governor Samuel B. Axtell addressed the Twenty-Second Session Territorial Legislative Assembly. In it he laid out his vision for New Mexico. He called for a revision of the territory's laws, stating, "Upon the very surface I find considerable confusion, and many incongruities in the Statutes. This is true of all new states. The tendency is to over legislate. The world is not only governed too much, but it has too many laws. We wish to prune down, simplify and codify the Statutes; make them so plain that all can understand them."[8] While his speech put forth his agenda for the territory, over the next few years his reliance on the advice of a few men and, in many cases, his failure to seek out both sides of an issue led to the belief that he was a part of, or being used by, the Santa Fe Ring.

Not long after, in Santa Fe, the territorial legislative assembly passed a bill attaching Colfax County to Taos County for judicial purposes because of the alleged anarchy in Colfax County. The bill passed on January 14, 1876, the last day of the legislative session. An editorial in the *Santa Fe Daily New Mexican* opined, "This legislation was demanded by reason of the lawlessness and anarchy that it is well known has existed in that county for several years, and has assumed a somewhat chronic form during the past year."[9] In Colfax County, however, public opinion was strong against the legislation. Colfax County citizens believed the bill not only sent the message that they were unfit to serve as jurors and decide their own cases but also brought about the hardship and hazard of having to travel fifty-five miles or more and over a mountain range—which was covered in snow for part of the year—to attend court in Taos. Not only that, but another result of the bill meant that the charges against Robert Longwill and Florencio Donoghue for their alleged involvement in planning the assassination of F. J. Tolby would not be heard by a grand jury composed of Colfax County citizens but by a grand jury composed of Taos County citizens. Could this have been a motive behind the annexation bill? Two days after the bill passed, Will Dawson, who was so recently accused of being a tool of the Santa Fe Ring because of his denunciation of the *New York Sun* letter, telegraphed Governor Axtell on Colfax County's behalf. The telegram read, "Don't sign Colfax and Taos Judiciary bill until you hear from the people of Colfax County." Three days later Axtell sent back a two-word reply: "Bill signed."[10]

On January 19 an invitation was sent to Axtell asking him to visit Colfax County. It was signed by William Morley, Henry M. Porter (a local merchant and a director for the Maxwell Land Grant and Railway Company), and W. C. Cunningham. It read, "Will you meet a convention of the people of the county to determine this Taos annexation question? Understanding you have power to annul the bill; if so, when?" Axtell replied, "The law requires two terms to be held in Taos. Should it then appear that its objects have been accomplished, the Governor is authorized to restore the courts to Colfax. All the assistance I can render law abiding citizens of your county in bringing law breakers to justice will be cheerfully rendered." In response to Axtell, William Morley sent the following telegram on January 29: "Like most troubles there are two sides; a speedy visit from you to Colfax would be best in my opinion." Axtell's reply: "I see two sides; broken laws, property wantonly destroyed and murdered men are on one side. I have no compromise to make with the other."[11]

Meanwhile, though Will Dawson took the side of the local citizenry on the issue of moving the court to Taos, the Cimarron *New and Press* under him was still seen by many as a mouthpiece for the Santa Fe Ring. To express their displeasure with the paper, on Wednesday night, January 19, a mob led by Clay Allison broke into the *New and Press* office, with one account having them using a log to bash in the door. Once inside the men used

Samuel Beach Axtell, circa 1881. Photographer unknown. Resource Identifier 000-742-0004, William A. Keleher Collection, Center for Southwest Research, University of New Mexico, Albuquerque, NM.

explosives to blow the press off its foundation. They took the press and type to the nearby bridge and threw it over into the river. Legend has it that Allison took the current edition, which so far had only been printed on one side, and wrote, in red letters, "Clay Allison's Edition" across the other side of every paper. The next morning, with Joe Curtis, who was part of the group that tossed the press into the river, Allison sold the papers around town.[12]

Back of *Cimarron News and Press* office, center, circa 1872. Photographer unknown. Norman Cleaveland Papers, Image #00250172, Rio Grande Historical Collections, New Mexico State University Archives and Special Collections, Las Cruces, NM.

A Morley family story, which Ada Morley told to her daughter, Agnes Morley Cleaveland, and grandson Norman Cleaveland, both of whom wrote of her recollection, said that on the night of the destruction of the press, Ada Morley (the Morleys were part owners of the paper), while she was getting ready for bed, heard the explosion from the *New and Press* office. According to her the press was blown from its foundation with a charge of black powder (which also did considerable damage to the office). Fearing something had happened to her husband, who had gone to see a neighbor, she rushed over to the neighbor's house, where she found him safe. The following morning she went to the office to view the damage. While she was there, Clay Allison came by to view his work. What he found was Ada Morley, seven months pregnant, standing in the office crying.[13] Morley turned to Allison and screamed at him. According to Ada's daughter, who wrote about this encounter many years later, Allison stammered, "Are you Mrs. Morley? Well, go buy yourself another printing press." Allison pulled out a "wrist-thick" roll of dollar bills and thrust them into her hand, saying, "I don't fight women."[14] The money he gave her may have been the proceeds from selling the paper. An angry, probably drunk, and armed Clay Allison wasn't likely to have had many refusals from those asked to purchase a copy, no matter what the asking price.

Ada Morley. Date and photographer unknown. Victor Grant Collection Photo
Albums, Arthur Johnson Memorial Library, Raton, NM.

Before Tolby's assassination, Allison had been antagonistic toward
William Morley, but the murder of F. J. Tolby had put the two men on the
same side of the Colfax County War, and after the destruction of the printing
press, there was no more trouble between them.[15]

Chapter 7

Dealing with
Colfax County

Following the demolition of the *News and Press* printing press, Will Dawson left the paper, which gave control back to Frank Springer and William Morley. After the announcement that Dawson was leaving, the partners published a statement addressing changes to the paper:

> Under the original management, some embarrassment was often occasioned by differences of opinion among the editors on subjects of public interest, and these differences finally culminated in a rupture, and thereafter, and for the past few weeks, the paper has not been in accord with the prevailing sentiment in the county. So obnoxious became the utterances in its columns, that a storm was aroused, which, in literal fact, shook the News and Press to its foundation, and the present proprietors suffered a severe loss in the destruction of the office, on account of something for which they were not in any way responsible.

Editors Springer and Morley promised that no more differences would "divert the force of this paper from its war upon the corruptions and abuses of rings, great and small, and the exposure of all the nefarious means for gaining and perpetuating power at the expense of the rights of the people." After pledging to be "independent upon all questions" and "conducted in the interest of no party, ring or clique," they closed, "There is little or no profit in publishing a newspaper in this country, but on the contrary, annoyance and trouble. But these are 'times that try men's souls,' and we feel it the duty of every citizen to come forward in whatever capacity he is best fitted, and join with his fellows in a united effort to extricate the county from the difficulties which envelope it. To this end a newspaper is a necessity, and we propose to furnish one to the best of our ability."[1] This issue of the *News and Press*, as well as the next few, were printed out of town while a press was reassembled.[2]

A good deal of lawlessness continued in and around Cimarron, at least according to Colfax County sheriff Orson K. Chittenden, who on January 21 wrote to Governor Axtell the short message, "It is impossible for me to enforce the civil law." Axtell's reply: "Will accept your resignation forwarded by mail." When no resignation was given, Axtell found a way to get rid of Chittenden. Judge Henry L. Waldo had conveniently refused to accept bonds given by the sheriff. This gave Axtell the excuse he needed to remove Chittenden from office. He was replaced with Isaiah Rinehart.[3] During this time Axtell wrote to President Grant to request the use of US Cavalry to make arrests and restore order in Colfax County. Axtell blamed all the trouble, and every murder, on Clay Allison, saying Allison headed a band of forty desperadoes. The governor charged that this gang had "committed many acts of violence in Cimarron" and wrote that in the past three months they had "murdered five men publicly [even if they receive blame for Vega and Cardenas along with Griego, that's only three]—have destroyed the printing Office and thrown the material into the river, have run out of the County the Probate Judge [Longwill,] the Justice of the Peace at Cimarron, some of the merchants and other peaceable citizens, and created such a terror in the minds of the people that no one will voluntarily appear to prosecute them before the Courts, nor even make an affidavit on which to found a warrant for their arrest."[4] Admitting there was no warrant for Allison's arrest, Axtell doesn't explain what he thought would happen to Allison after his arrest. Later correspondence suggests Axtell's goal may have been the death of Clay Allison at the hands of the military.

With Axtell in Santa Fe, and the messages from Colfax County residents having no effect, Frank Springer traveled to Santa Fe to make a personal

Palace of the Governors, Santa Fe, circa 1878. Photographer unknown. Author's collection.

appeal to Axtell to restore the courts to Colfax County. Springer was allowed to meet with Axtell in the governor's office.

Springer later described the meeting during a deposition, stating that he "endeavored to show to the Governor that there was no cause for" the annexation of Colfax County to Taos for judicial purposes, "and that the vast majority of the inhabitants of Colfax County were good, law-abiding citizens." He said he "urged the Governor to go to Colfax County and examine the situation for himself." According to Springer Axtell responded that he

> absolutely refused to visit Colfax County, saying that he had visited the other counties in the Territory, for the purpose of seeing the people, and getting acquainted with them, and learning their wants, but that he should not go to Colfax County until the people showed a different disposition. Said Axtell was, during this conversation, very bitter in his allusions to the people of Colfax County, and especially in his allusions to one R. C. Allison, whom he denounced as a murderer, and who, he said, was guilty of several murders both in Colfax County and other parts of the Territory, and declared that he (Axtell) was going to have him indicted and punished for all of them, or else compel him to leave the country.[5]

When Springer returned to Colfax County, he informed others about his meeting with Axtell and, with "twelve or fifteen citizens," prepared and sent an invitation to the governor asking him to visit Colfax County to "see for himself the true condition of affairs." Signatories included Springer, Morley, and Clay Allison. According to Springer Axtell did not send a response.[6]

Things started looking up for those wanting Axtell to visit when, on about the first day of March, Frank Springer, while in Las Vegas, New Mexico, was told by Benjamin Stevens, district attorney for New Mexico's second judicial district, that he, Stevens, was going to visit Cimarron. He did just that a few days later.[7]

William R. Morley, who was acquainted with Stevens, said of his stop in Cimarron that Stevens "displayed considerable interest in Colfax County matters," and that after staying for "two or three days," he was "satisfied the people of Colfax County had been very much misrepresented." Morley believed Stevens "would go back and see the Governor and try and induce him to" go "to Colfax County and see the people and learn the facts for himself."[8]

Stevens left Cimarron. He did not meet with Axtell during the time he was away but did correspond with the governor about the Colfax situation. Stevens returned to Cimarron in mid-March, arriving at the same time as a company of soldiers from Fort Union under the command of Captain Francis Moore. Moore said he was there at the request of Stevens.

Back in Cimarron, Stevens showed Morley a telegram he had received from Axtell, which read,

Do not let it be known that I will be in Cimarron on Saturday's coach. Body Guard all right.

                                                          S. B. Axtell[9]

Stevens told Morley the governor did not want it "generally known" that he would be in Cimarron, and said that Axtell "felt much more kindly toward the people of Colfax County than before, and that he was anxious to meet them and talk with them." He added that Axtell "wanted to see one R. C. Allison particularly, as he believed he had been greatly misrepresented." He reiterated that Axtell did not want the meeting "generally known because he did not want a crowd," but that he wanted Morley, Allison, and a "few others" who signed the invitation to Axtell to be there.[10]

Later that same day, Morley was informed of the contents of another letter Axtell had sent Stevens. It was later suggested that, after he had been drinking, Stevens was the source of this information. What Morley learned about the letter made him believe there was a plot to have him and others "killed under color of an attempt to arrest some person on a fictitious charge." Morley informed the others who were to attend the meeting of what he learned. Nobody showed up for Axtell's arrival, which worked out because the governor never came.[11]

The possibility that the governor of the territory planned the killing of several citizens surely became a topic of conversation for Morley, Springer, Allison, and others with knowledge of this, but, without proof, word of the alleged plot stayed among a few for the time being.

Soon after, Clay Allison was arrested at his ranch with soldiers as part of the arresting party. Allison gave no resistance and was brought to town, detained for a few hours, and then set free. The troops then returned to Fort Union.[12] A report from Captain Francis Moore gives a different view of Allison than the one held by Governor Axtell: "Allison[']s reputation here is that of a man of property and no outlaw, and his principle friends here are men of means—the largest property holders in the county."[13]

Days after Allison's arrest, on March 24, there were gunshots once again in Cimarron—this time unrelated to land grants disagreements, the Santa Fe Ring, or the Tolby murder. Three troops, who were part of the detachment under Moore, were in Lambert's Saloon in the St. James Hotel. The soldiers—John Hanson, Anthony Harvey, and George Small—were leaving the saloon when Texans Gus Heffron and David (Davy) Crockett (a relative of the Davy who died at the Alamo) were entering. Crockett was drunk and is said by some to have begun shooting at the three US soldiers simply because they were Black. A gunfight erupted and all three soldiers were killed. Following the senseless murders, Heffron and Crockett rode out of town and disappeared for months.[14]

Chapter 8

Term of Court

The citizens of Colfax County who had been summoned to appear in court made the nearly sixty-mile journey to Taos toward the end of April 1876. Axtell had troops on the scene, for he feared that "bodies of armed men from Colfax Co. will be present at Taos."[1] His fears proved unfounded. The grand jury that would be hearing the cases was selected by Pedro Sanchez of Taos, president of the New Mexico Legislative Assembly Council and reliable member of the Santa Fe Ring.[2] When court opened the presiding judge, Chief Justice Henry Waldo, instructed the grand jury regarding the Colfax County cases as follows:

> At the last session of the Territorial Assembly the neighboring county of Colfax was annexed to Taos County, for Judicial purposes. . . . During a period of time dating no further back than the first of November last, no less than eight homicides have been committed in the town of Cimarron or its immediate vicinity, and since the beginning of the year 1875 at least 16 or 18 men have come to their deaths in brawls or by assassination to say nothing of numerous shootings and woundings of which but little note has been taken. It is a matter of shameful and horrid notoriety, at which all decent men may well stand shocked, that one room [Lambert's Saloon] alone in the village of Cimarron, can

Taos Plaza, 1880. The courthouse is the large building with the pitched roof in the middle of the block on the right. Photographer unknown. Negative #014820, Palace of the Governors Photo Archives, Santa Fe, NM (NMHM/DCA).

> boast that not less than six men have been killed within its walls, during the last nine months, besides having been the scene of many fierce and bloody rencounters not ending in death. It is perhaps no exaggeration to say that there is hardly a plank in its floor, but that could it speak, would tell some fearful tale of blood. Such a record of crime is appalling to the imagination and a disgrace to the civilization of the age and of the country in which we live.[3]

The grand jury met for two weeks. Robert "Clay" Allison had seven indictments brought against him: three for murder for the deaths of Charles Cooper, Chunk Colbert, and Francisco Griego. Why charges for the killings of Colbert and Cooper were brought now was never explained. Allison had killed Colbert over two years earlier in what was clearly self-defense. Charles Cooper, who not only witnessed the Colbert killing but also had been shot in the hand by Colbert, disappeared less than two weeks later and, for reasons now unknown, some suspected Allison had killed him, though it wasn't even known whether Cooper was dead or had just left the area. The range of charges brought against Allison makes it

Chief Justice Henry Waldo. Date and photographer unknown. Resource Identifier 000-021-0163, Miguel Antonio Otero Photograph Collection, Center for Southwest Research, University of New Mexico, Albuquerque, NM.

appear there was a desire to pin some crime—any crime—on him. He was never put on trial for any of the seven indictments brought against him. Oscar McMains, along with many others, was indicted for "planning the lynching" of Cruz Vega.[4] As for the murder of Reverend Franklin J. Tolby, the grand jury reported:

> The fullest investigation which the grand jury could make was given to the charges made against Mills, Longwill and Donoghue; and all persons who were supposed to have any knowledge of the facts, as far as the grand jury could learn, were brought before it and thoroughly examined, being permitted to tell what they knew; and after a very careful examination the grand jury was unable to discover the least evidence which implicated either of the persons above named in the assassination; the charges brought against them, as far as the grand jury could ascertain, being based solely on rumors and suspicions. From the evidence placed before the grand jury it appears that the only persons who it is reasonable to suppose had any knowledge of the assassination, were themselves murdered while in the custody of persons ostensibly engaged in an investigation to discover the facts about Mr. Tolby's murder.[5]

While it is certainly understandable that there were no indictments against Mills, Longwill, and Donoghue, to characterize the accusations against them as "being based solely on rumors and suspicions" is incorrect. Manuel Cardenas, in a signed statement, claimed that Longwill, Mills, and Donoghue, along with Francisco Griego, paid to have Tolby killed. While this is hardly enough on its own to indict anyone of a crime, it is more than rumor and suspicion. Furthermore, the grand jury's claim that "it appears that the only persons who it is reasonable to suppose had any knowledge of the assassination, were themselves murdered" is a complete falsehood. The finding ignores the complete lack of motive for Cardenas or Vega to kill Tolby on their own accord. There was no evidence that either man had a personal reason to want Tolby dead, and nothing was taken from him, so robbery wasn't the reason for the murder. While the evidence may not show beyond a reasonable doubt who induced Vega and Cardenas to kill Tolby, there can be no doubt that the idea to assassinate Reverend Tolby did not originate with those two.

Putting this misrepresentation of the evidence by the grand jury aside, the actions of excited citizens of Colfax County in attempting to bring to justice anyone behind the murder of F. J. Tolby unfortunately made their decision to not indict anyone for planning Tolby's assassination inevitable. While it is possible that it wasn't Colfax men who gunned down Manuel Cardenas, Cruz Vega was killed by men avenging Tolby's murder. By luring Vega out to that cornfield, Oscar McMains had Vega forever silenced. Three years after Tolby's murder, Reverend Thomas Harwood commented on the strong feeling and dangerous environment the murder had caused, and how McMains had negatively impacted the situation. Harwood recalled, "The country was thrown into a fearful condition and at times it seemed with the light of a match it might set the whole country ablaze." Reverend McMains, Harwood believed, only made things worse. Of McMains Harwood wrote, "He was often rash, often imprudent, not safe as a leader, and too strong to be led; but in the main he meant well. He had the faculty of getting himself and others into trouble much easier than he could get us out." Of the effect McMains had on the mood in New Mexico, Harwood said, "The excitement and danger were greatly intensified by the unwise efforts upon the part of the Rev. O. P. McMains who spent much time in trying to ferret out the case and bring the guilty parties to arrest." Of how McMains affected the investigation, Harwood opined that "the unwise methods of Mr. McMains served to cover up the tracks of evidence and they have never been found."[6]

Oscar P. McMains was back in Colfax County when he received word that he had been indicted. He traveled to Cimarron and surrendered. He was placed in the small, freestanding jail in Cimarron. Also incarcerated there for the same charge were William H. Terhune and Jimmy Thorpe.[7] Friends of McMains raised money for his defense and hired Frank Springer as his attorney. Springer filed a writ of habeas corpus and Judge Henry Waldo set a hearing for May 25 in Santa Fe. McMains, along with 24-year-old William Terhune, who also had a hearing scheduled before the court, were brought to Santa Fe.

At the hearing the defense did not address the charges against McMains and Terhune, instead arguing against the legality of indictments brought by a grand jury composed exclusively of Taos citizens, emphasizing that the jury had been selected during the September term of court, which was before the annexation law even passed. The argument didn't work. Bail for Terhune and McMains was set at $20,000 each.[8] With bail set so high, McMains went right back to jail. He was also suspended from his missionary work.

During his stay in jail, McMains received frequent visitors, including the Morleys and Clay Allison, who was out of jail but still under indictment. William Morley once brought his daughter, Agnes, to receive a bow and arrow McMains had made for her. McMains was even let out occasionally to do things such as going to dinner at the Morley home (a short walk from the jail), where, two months earlier, William Morley and his wife Ada celebrated good news with the birth of their second child, William Raymond Jr.

That summer William Morley would leave the struggling Maxwell Land Grant and Railway Company and take a job with the Denver and Rio Grande Railway. A year later he moved on to the employ of the Atchison, Topeka, and Santa Fe Railway. During these career changes, the Morley family remained in Cimarron.[9]

Meanwhile, in early June 1876, Clay Allison shared a coach from Vermejo, Colfax County, to Trinidad, Colorado, with Governor Samuel Axtell. It may have been a planned meeting between the two men to discuss the allegations of murder and mayhem Axtell made against Allison. Frank Springer, who was not present, claimed the coach ride was the result of an

Cimarron, circa 1890. The jail is the building surrounded by a stone wall on the left. The porch of the Maxwell Land Grant and Railway Company Head-quarters, where the Morleys lived, is right of center. Photographer unknown. Old Aztec Mill Museum, Cimarron, NM.

appointment the governor made with the gunfighter to discuss the murder charges against him. According to Springer's version, "Gov Axtell made an appointment with him, met him at Vermejo station, in Colfax County, and traveled with him in a friendly way for some fifty miles."[10] Axtell remembered it differently. He was traveling in the public stagecoach on the first part of a trip to Philadelphia to take part in the Centennial Exhibition (World's Fair) when he shared the ride with Allison. Axtell said of Allison boarding the stagecoach,

> when we arrived on the Vermejo in Colfax county, where the coach stopped to change the mail, Mr. Allison came to the coach and took passage for Trinidad. The coach was full of passengers, among them Mr. Wilson Waddingham of New York city, who can probably recollect all that took place. What Mr. Springer supposes, although sworn to by him is entirely the product of a diseased imagination; I say again and for fear you may over look it will put it in a different form of expression: Mr. Springer's statement that I had an appointment to meet Mr. Allison is a lie.[11]

However, giving more credence to Springer's claim is a statement from William D. Lee, who said that Allison and Axtell had an appointment to meet at his house. He saw Allison first near his house, and Allison told him he'd be at a nearby store. Shortly after Axtell arrived in Cimarron and came to Lee's house asking for Allison. Axtell and Lee went to the store to see Allison, where, according to Lee, Axtell met "Allison very cordially, shook hands, and secured for Allison a seat in the coach, which was crowded, and they went away together in the coach. One of the passengers took a seat on the outside of the coach, to make room for Allison beside the Governor."[12]

Life in Cimarron was peaceful in the summer of 1876—until the return of David Crockett and Gus Heffron. The men had returned to town before the opening of the September term of court to answer for Crockett's murdering of three soldiers the previous March. In yet another example of murder going unpunished in Cimarron, the only charge brought against either of them was Crockett being charged with illegally carrying a firearm, a charge of which he'd be found guilty and fined $50.[13] Emboldened by getting away with murder, Crockett and Heffron returned during the second half of September hell-bent on causing terror. One citizen wrote to the *Santa Fe Daily New Mexican,* "We have had quite a lively time in and around Cimarron for the last two weeks, caused by two men, Dave Crockett and Gus Heffron, undertaking to "run the town.""[14] And another citizen, years later, remembered the final day of their rampage: "They came to town one day, got drunk as usual, and proceeded to shoot up the town, riding up and down the streets shooting and yelling."[15] That was September 30, when Sheriff Isaiah Rinehart, with deputy Joseph Holbrook and John B. McCullough, attempted to arrest the men. Crockett and Heffron, both on horseback, responded by going for their guns. The lawmen fired, and shots hit both Crockett and Heffron. The two took off and the lawmen gave chase. On the north side of the river, Crockett collapsed and died from his wounds. Heffron was arrested but escaped from custody on October 31.[16]

Chapter 9

Mary McPherson

On October 10, 1876, Frank Springer married Josephine Bishop. Taking a honeymoon trip east, the newlyweds stopped in Indianapolis in November, where Frank Springer met with William Fishbank to discuss the McMains case. Fishbank was not only the brother-in-law of Oscar McMains but also a powerful attorney with political connections. In October Mary McPherson also stopped in Indianapolis to see Fishbank, but he was out of town at the time so she wrote him a letter. In St. Louis, Indianapolis, and Washington, McPherson worked to get the support of the Methodist Church for McMains. A few months after she began this, McMains wrote to McPherson asking her to stop, saying he did not believe it would help him, and adding, "your representations of the way they talk humiliates me."[1]

Meanwhile, Clay Allison had trouble unrelated to the Colfax County affairs when he and his brother John were in Las Animas, Colorado. On December 21 the Allison brothers were in town and, according to reports, were drinking and causing trouble. Said the *Colorado Chieftain*, "The Allisons were both drunk, going around the hall [Olympic Dance Hall] and trying to provoke a fight. They insulted men they never saw before, and went so far as to amuse themselves by tramping on the toes of the bystanders."[2]

Frank and Josephine Springer, 1876. Taken in Burlington, Iowa, by Montfort & Hill. Frank Springer Collection, CS Cattle Company, Cimarron, NM.

Earlier in the day, constable Charles Faber had attempted to disarm Clay and John, but the men refused to give up their guns and the constable didn't press the matter. That night, at the Olympic Dance Hall, after dancing in the same set as the Allisons, Faber left the hall. He returned with two unidentified men to assist him in arresting the troublemakers. Faber had his shotgun aimed toward the Allison brothers when someone shouted, "Look out!" At that moment, with no other warning, Faber fired, hitting John Allison. The shot knocked John to the ground. Clay quickly drew his pistol and shot Faber. As Faber—killed by the gunshot—fell, the second barrel of his shotgun discharged, hitting the already wounded John Allison. The two men with Faber fled. Allison rushed through the doors and took a few shots at the running deputies but failed to connect. He then returned to his ailing brother, who had buckshot in his breast and leg. Some of the buckshot that entered John Allison's breast was later removed from his back.[3]

Sheriff John Spiers arrested the brothers Allison at the Vandiver House, a hotel, shortly after the shooting and took them to the West Las Animas jail. Clay was held on $10,000 bail for the death of Charles Faber. At the hearing Judge John W. Henry said the evidence pointed to no crime greater than manslaughter. John Allison, as he continued his recovery, was released for lack of evidence. He survived his wounds. In March the grand jury brought no charges against Clay Allison and he was released.[4] Around this time he sold his interest in the Allison ranch to John. Clay Allison left New Mexico in 1878 and would no longer be a player in the Colfax County troubles.[5]

While Clay and John Allison were in Colorado, Mary McPherson moved her fight to help Oscar McMains and expose the corruption in New Mexico to Washington, DC. She arrived at the capital just before the start of the presidency of Republican Rutherford B. Hayes and worked tirelessly to lobby the new administration. On February 28, 1877, a friend of McPherson, Emma Hunt, wrote to her to update her on the situation in New Mexico and on how McMains was doing. Of McMains Hunt wrote, "Judge [William D.] Lee and wife, Pa and Ma, and Mr. McMains took dinner with Mr. Morley's [sic] two days ago. Spent the day,—had music and lots of talk. Mr. McMains is out a great deal now."[6]

About the same time, McPherson wrote to her daughter and son-in-law to let them know about her progress. In reply William Morley wrote, "I was astonished beyond measure, at your proceedings, and have fears as to the result: at the same time I will not throw a straw in your way, but will do what I can to help matters." He updated her on the fight in New Mexico, and then gave his opinion about all that had transpired:

Efforts have been made to get the court back here, but failed. The Ring will not permit it, and say that the objects for which the court was taken away have not been accomplished; You know what the objects were,— to defeat the Tolby investigation, and to punish Colfax County for

Mary McPherson. Date and photographer unknown. Norman Cleaveland
Papers, Image #00250005, Rio Grande Historical Collections New Mexico
State University Archives and Special Collections, Las Cruces, NM.

presuming to interfere in such matters. I have to go to court the last of
this month,—and you know what a Taos court is. The election of [Pres-
ident Rutherford B.] Hayes leads many to think that the old regime
will hold over, and that other Tolby affairs will happen. The people are
badly discouraged, and many talk of leaving the country, as their only
protection against the machinations of their enemies in power. . . . If
you can effect any removals, you will certainly do good. Four or five
men run this Territory, and run it with unparalleled desperation. . . .

The removal of one or two, even, of these officials would remedy
the great evil; provided men were in their places who could not be
controlled by the Ring. . . . The Mormon schemes alone ought to
remove Axtell.

The "Mormon schemes" Morley referred to was an allegation that Axtell
planned to help Mormons take over large parts of New Mexico Territory

Washington, DC, Pennsylvania Avenue from US Treasury, circa 1880. Reproduction number: LC-USZ62-59101, Library of Congress Prints and
Photographs Division, Library of Congress, Washington, DC.

for Mormon settlement. The allegation grew out of the friendly relationship Axtell had with Mormons when he was the governor of Utah and a
letter he had written the *Salt Lake Herald* praising New Mexico. The claim
was absurd and there was no evidence to support it. Following the Mormon
nonsense, Morley circled back to his hope that they could get the removal
of a Ringite from office, but wrote that the only way to accomplish this
would be "if a secret agent were to come here *duly authorized*, he could
get them,—get evidence to astonish the world! But people are afraid to tell
what they know in affidavits until they feel sure it will not pass into the
hands of the enemy to be used against themselves." Morley opined, "Effect
one removal,—the Governor, or, Chief Justice, and if a Governor could be
appointed who knew the circumstances here, it would be best,—*any good,
square man would do.*"[7]

McPherson's daughter wrote her the following day to give her opinion about McPherson's work in Washington and update her on the situation in New Mexico:

> I have little hope of your being able to cause any removals for you know the Republicans have gained the day and our *exRebels* [meaning former southern Democrats] here are the finest Republicans in New Mexico. . . . I am really afraid to write on these matters. Elkins of course is there trying to keep his friends in their present positions and as I said I have little hope or faith that you can succeed. . . . You know what they have done and that McMains is to be tried in three weeks and *I'm sure* they will convict him though hes [sic] innocent as Agnes of murder. I am half crazy too because Raym must go to be tried—it will cost a hundred dollars then he will likely be indicted again for something—and I often think they'll manage to kill him in some way or other. If they do I'd not be a second Mrs. Tolby. They'd hear from me. . . . Every body here is discouraged and disheartened. All that I see you can do is to have an Agent sent but a secret one. He could see & hear and learn all.

Ada Morley expressed concern about money, told her mother that they couldn't help her financially because they didn't even have enough money to cover their own debts, and suggested if she could find a way to earn money she should take it. Ada also worried that if McPherson failed Raymond "will have to take the blows" for what she did, but acknowledged, "Should you succeed what a glorious and great blessing it would be for this God forsaken country." Morley defined success as getting "an investigation or an Agent or something to turn attention this way." Ada Morley then turned to more personal issues,

> I have some good news to write[.] McMains was here for dinner yesterday (as Burleson lets him out in town) and he says Senator [Henry] *Teller* of Colorado is a personal and warm friend of his, and that his wife is a leading methodist and they can be of immense help to him. . . . Rayms [sic] health is only fair. He has quit smoking. I think [he] is less nervous now[.] He has changed so much in some ways. Willie loves him and he can do as much with Agnes as I. Is in every way good and devoted to his family. I wish you could see him. We are a loving and happy family—All well.[8]

Mary McPherson then began addressing letters to people in positions of real power in Washington and they paid attention. She sent charges and evidence to President Hayes and Secretary of the Interior Carl Schurz. McPherson and William B. Matchett—an attorney she picked up along the way to help her cause—laid out the charges they alleged against Axtell in detail to Secretary of the Interior Schurz. Their first charge against Axtell was that he was connected "with a corrupt combination of men in procuring the enactment of laws inimical to the interests of the people of the Territory, and especially of Colfax County." To support the charge they focused on the removal of Colfax County courts to Taos County, writing that this deprived Colfax County citizens "of the right to a speedy and impartial trial by a jury of their own countrymen, and in the district where the crimes charged were alleged to have been committed." They also addressed the practical hardships brought about by the measure: "This removal of the Court compelled all persons charged with crime, or, as witnesses, to leave their avocations and travel some of them fifty to one hundred and fifty miles, over and beyond a ridge of mountains ten thousand feet in height and now covered with snow—encamping en route—to attend said court, upon pain of fine or imprisonment for refusal." They went on to tell how "principal citizens" invited Axtell to visit Colfax County to learn the true state of affairs in the county for himself, but that Axtell refused.[9]

The second charge leveled against Axtell was that he colluded with the same group of corrupt men for the purpose of reducing "large private grants of land to public domain, with a view to private gain, and, to induce settlements thereon of the people known as 'Latter Day Saints,' or, 'Mormons,'—from the adjoining Territory of Utah,—to the detriment of progress, and the peace and security of persons and property, of all good and law-abiding citizens of New Mexico." They wrote a lot about the ludicrous Mormon charge. Included is the copy of a letter Axtell wrote to the *Salt Lake Herald*. The letter, which trumpeted the resources and beauty of New Mexico, was seen by some as a recommendation to Utah Mormons to settle in, or take over, large parts of New Mexico. The anti-Axtell crowd also saw his signing the letter "El Obispo" as evidence that he was a bishop in the Church of Jesus Christ of Latter-day Saints.[10] They'd press this further when Matchett received a letter from Charles M. Howard, in which Howard repeated secondhand information that Brigham Young, president of the Church of Jesus Christ of Latter-day Saints, had baptized Axtell into the Mormon Church. Brigham Young had to write a letter stating that he never baptized Axtell and that Axtell was not a bishop in the church. As for Axtell signing the letter "El Obispo," Axtell later explained, "I formed while in Utah, a pleasant acquaintance with the Editors of the Herald, and some one had facetiously styled me 'the Bishop,' and in writing for the Press, I have sometimes adopted 'El Obispo' the Spanish for 'the Bishop' as a *nom de Plume*."[11] Matchett and McPherson closed, "Accompanying are letters and papers from citizens of the Territory, which we put in evidence, and request, in behalf of the people of the territory the earliest attention of the government to the matter."[12]

While there wasn't any immediate action taken on the charges they made against New Mexico officials, the efforts on behalf of Oscar McMains resulted in a request from United States attorney general Charles Devens to New Mexico attorney general William Breeden to suspend the proceedings against McMains. This was refused. On the broader issue of the Colfax court annexation, Solicitor General Samuel Phillips (of the Department of Justice) gave the opinion that the Taos court could not indict and try defendants from Colfax County. New Mexican officials declined to follow the opinion and cases went ahead.[13]

Chapter 10

Axtell Responds

Secretary of the Interior Carl Schurz wrote to Axtell on May 11, 1877, to inform him of the allegations against him and asked for a response. The governor wrote a brief reply on May 20 stating that he was not a Mormon and, regarding the signing of the bill attaching Colfax County to Taos for judicial purposes, Axtell wrote, "I have no interest to act otherwise than for the public good."[1]

Axtell followed that with a more detailed response to Schurz on June 14 in which he said all the charges made against him were false. He denied that he was a Mormon or secret agent of Brigham Young and said there was no truth to the allegation that he was preparing New Mexico for a massive Mormon settlement. In his closing comment about the Mormon claims, Axtell correctly pointed out, "If the people referred to, have any purpose or intention of coming to New Mexico, I know of nothing that could be done, or that would be necessary to prepare the way, as their [sic] is nothing to prevent, and no obstacle to their coming, if they chose to come." As to the more serious charges of conspiring with the Santa Fe Ring, Axtell declared, "It is absolutely untrue that I have connected myself with a corrupt combination of men, forming a powerful ring, to procure legislation by the Territorial Assembly of New Mexico, in the interests of said ring and inimical to the interests of the people of the Territory. I am not and never have been connected with a corrupt combination of men or ring, for any purpose. I know of no such combination in this Territory and if such a one exists, I am certainly in no wise connected with it or privy to its operations, and purposes." Regarding the law attaching Colfax County to Taos for judicial purposes, Axtell wrote, "I had no connection with the measure or part in its passage except, that I signed and approved the law. I had not and have not, any doubt that the legislature acted in the matter from entirely proper motives and believed that the action was peremptorily required by the condition of affairs in Colfax County and that it was absolutely necessary to secure the enforcement of the laws and the security of life and property in Colfax County." He said he preferred to leave the decision to restore the courts to Colfax to the legislative assembly. Axtell closed by defending his decision not to have made "a formal visit to Colfax County," writing, "I have twice been through the county and have been well informed as to matters of public interest transpiring there and there has been no time when I believed that my presence in that County would subserve the public interests in any way."[2]

That same month Elkins came to Axtell's defense. On June 11 Elkins sent a letter to President Hayes saying that he heard Axtell's removal as the governor of New Mexico was under consideration. Ekins wrote that "the bonafide citizens, property holders & good people without distinction of party heartily endorse him, and believe him to be a worthy and efficient officer." As to the allegations made against Axtell, Elkins claimed, "The charges filed against him in the Interior Department are for the most part vague & indefinite, and so far as certain are absolutely false. They are prefered [sic] by . . . non-residents who have no interest in the Territory & to satisfy a few bad people to whom I am informed the Governor gave offence in attempting to repress violence and murder."[3]

More Axtell supporters came to his defense with a petition to President Hayes while others appealed to First Assistant Secretary of the Treasury Richard C. McCormick to help save Axtell's job. William Breeden wrote to McCormick about Axtell, "the Territory never had a Governor who exerted himself so much to make himself acquainted with the wants, necessities, character & capability of the Country and people."[4]

Axtell didn't help himself among detractors when business took him to Colfax County. Axtell went to the county with Arkansas senator Stephen Dorsey to examine the Uña de Gato grant, which Dorsey was interested in purchasing. Axtell again refused an invitation to visit with citizens while passing through Cimarron.[5] Axtell later defended his decision, saying he preferred "to sleep in the open plain" rather than step foot in Cimarron. Axtell stated bluntly, "I cannot understand how any right minded man could do otherwise; the place [Cimarron] is crimson with human blood and polluted with the hourly presence of liars, slanderers and murderers. I have never heard that charges were preferred against Lot because he would not stay in Sodom."[6]

On July 26 Matchett and McPherson wrote to Secretary of the Interior Schurz and sent him letters, petitions, and other documents to support their charges against Axtell.[7] They also began collecting affidavits to strengthen their case. The affidavits didn't just concern Axtell. On July 31, 1877, Lewis Kingman, a United States deputy surveyor, gave evidence that the Uña de Gato grant was based on forged papers. It was eventually proven that Kingman was correct.[8] In another affidavit John L. Taylor claimed to have secondhand information about people arrested in San Miguel County, alleging that many of them agreed to vote for Stephen B. Elkins as part of the deal to gain their release.[9]

In the fall of 1875, Elkins resigned as president of the Maxwell Land Grant and Railway Company, though he still might have held considerable stock in the company at this time. His resignation may have been because he was scheming with good friend Tom Catron to seize the entire grant. The Maxwell Land Grant and Railway Company was dealing with money problems and the continuing question about the size of the grant. In December 1876, because the company had unpaid taxes, the property was auctioned off. Melvin Mills, working as a middleman for Thomas B. Catron, gained control of the property for $16,479; however, New Mexico law allowed for a redemption period, during which time the Maxwell Land Grant Company paid the taxes and were able to keep the land.[10]

In June 1877, following a Supreme Court decision that overruled a lower court's decision to limit Mexican land grants to only eleven leagues per grantee, Stephen Elkins sent a letter to the Interior Department requesting the Maxwell Land Grant boundaries be reinstated to those of the original survey commissioned by Maxwell and Chaffee. The request was rejected. Elkins followed this by asking for a new survey, and suggested that the field notes and plats from the original survey be used as a guide. The new survey was agreed to. On June 28 James A. Williamson wrote to Henry M. Atkinson, the surveyor general of New Mexico, asking him to choose a "disinterested deputy" with "no connection" to the grant's owners to do the survey. He chose two surveyors. One "disinterested deputy" Atkinson chose was John T. Elkins, brother of Stephen Elkins. The other surveyor was Walter G. Marmon.[11]

Chapter 11

The Trial of
Oscar P. McMains

Oscar McMains raised bail in June 1877 and resumed his ministry.[1] He was said to be in good spirits at the time and confident he'd be acquitted. The trial of O. P. McMains for his part in the death of Cruz Vega began on Wednesday, August 22, 1877, in Mora, New Mexico, with Attorney General William Breeden prosecuting the case and Frank Springer, with William D. Lee, representing McMains.

For the prosecution, Isaiah Rinehart, who had been on the coroner's jury, stated that he saw Vega's body by the telegraph pole the morning after the murder. Rinehart said, "We then examined him, and as well as I can recollect, the hind part of his head was all broken in like as though it had been done by some blunt instrument. We also found a bullet hole, but I can't recollect now if it was on the left side or the right side of his breast. The bullet also passed through behind, for we stripped him and found that the bullet went through; examined and also found that he had been hung." The questions turned to Rinehart's interactions with McMains. Rinehart testified that about a week before Vega's death, McMains came to his house and asked Rinehart if he thought Vega had murdered Tolby. Rinehart responded that all the evidence showed he was near Tolby when the murder occurred. McMains

Mora County Courthouse, Mora, New Mexico, 1904. Photographer unknown. Negative #001617, Palace of the Governors Photo Archives, Santa Fe, NM (NMHM/DCA).

asked Rinehart if he could get Vega out to the Ponil River so he could be questioned. Rinehart said he could not do that. Knowing the risk such a plan would pose to Vega, Rinehart said he told McMains "that if I would take him out there and something would happen to him that I would have to leave the country; that I could not do anything to convince the Mexicans but that it was my fault." At a later conversation, Rinehart testified that

McMains told him "that he was sorry that there was nobody there brave enough to bring Cruz Vega out to the Ponil," and McMains added that he was going to take it upon himself to get Vega out there for questioning. Under cross-examination, Rinehart said that Reverend Thomas Harwood was also at his home on the morning of the first conversation referred to, but that Harwood did not witness it. Of the second conversation, Rinehart said that Simeon Welding and a man named Phelps may have witnessed it. During reexamination Rinehart said, "I proposed to take Cruz Vega into a private room and tell him that the murder had been traced to him, and try to induce him to make a confession. To this the defendant said, 'that won't do.'"[2]

William Low, who was in custody, having also been charged with Vega's murder, was called to testify. Low stated that he last saw Cruz Vega on the night he was killed. Said Low, "I knew how he came to be at the Ponil that night. It was some time ago and I may make some mistakes, but I will tell it the best I know how. Mr. McMains wanted to get him out . . . to see if he couldn't find out who murdered Tolby." Of McMains planning to question Vega, Low testified, "Mr. McMains came to me one evening and he allowed I could take out Cruz Vega better than anyone else because I could talk a little Mexican. He said, 'I want him to confess. He must know something about that affair. He carried the mail down that day from Elizabethtown. If you can get him out, I don't want the man hurt, and won't have him hurt in any manner whatever. All I want of him is to get him to confess what he knows.'" Low said he had a crop of corn and suggested he hire Vega to guard the corn. McMains agreed to that and Low hired Vega for three nights. It was on the second night, a Saturday, that McMains and others came for Vega. Low related,

> We built a little fire close to the corn. It was chilly. Me and Cruz stayed there a while, maybe an hour, hour and a half or two hours. I dropped to sleep. Think Cruz Vega was asleep at the time. Some men came—four or six I think—went up to us and woke us up. Got up and so did Cruz. One of 'em said, 'hello boys,' and he walked up towards Cruz with a lariat [a lasso] and put it around his neck and said, 'come on,' and they took him along the road, took me with them in the road.[3]

Low said they went to a telegraph line that was "among the timber" where forty to fifty men were waiting. Low testified, "As soon as we came there these men—four or five—took him to the telegraph pole of their own accord. None of the other party said a word. The other party stood off one side." Low was told to leave, but decided to "run a little risk" and watch the proceedings. McMains, who was standing fifteen to twenty steps from the telegraph pole, called out questions to be asked. Low stated,

> Cruz Vega said something—have forgotten now what he did say. One of the men—one of the four or five standing by the telegraph pole— climbed the telegraph pole and put the rope over the wire, and they raised him up on their own accord and hung him up. They kept him up a few seconds and let him down again, then Mr. McMains told them what questions to ask. He said I believe all that they wanted to hear. Then these four or five, whoever they were—it was dark—they stayed with Cruz Vega. The other party, Mr. McMains and the balance of the party, held a little conversation with each other. They got on their horses and started towards town.[4]

Low said he followed the men who left from a distance. They crossed the bridge over the Ponil River, then Low, for some reason he didn't explain, waded through the river. He returned to the house he was staying at—the same place McMains was boarding. In the morning Low found McMains crying. Their conversation, according to Low, was as follows:

Low asked, "Mr. McMains what's up now?"

McMains responded, "Did you hear that shooting last night?"

"Yes, I did, but I don't suppose they killed the man, did they?"

"I don't know," said McMains. He continued, "I came away last night and I found out I had no control over the men and I left." Low offered to return to the scene and see if they had killed Vega, but quickly changed his mind and said he would go to town and tell people what happened. McMains, still crying, responded, "Do whatever you please about it."

Low said he went to town and told "everybody" what he had seen, then, at about 9:00 am he went with Sheriff Chittenden to Vega's body. Low was questioned again about the night of the murder. He said, "It was close about 9 o'clock in the night when the things mentioned occurred." Low said the events he described took place over an hour to an hour and a half and stated it was another hour to an hour and a half from when he left until he heard the shot that ended the life of Cruz Vega. Low stated that "every one of the party that came near enough for me to see was disguised—had something on his face. It was pretty dark to me—have only got one eye." About McMains Low added, "Can't say if McMains was disguised because it was dark. Went up to McMains and says to him, 'Where is McMains?' and he said, 'This is me.'"[5]

The next witness to take the stand was Irvin Lacy. He was asked about a conversation he had with McMains after Vega was murdered. He said McMains had told him about the plan to have Low hire Vega to guard his corn. Lacy testified, "Low was to take Vega to this place and build a fire there as a signal for these men to know that he was there." Lacy clarified that by "these men," he meant "the men McMains said he had under his direction." McMains told Lacy that a small part of the group went to get Vega and bring him to them. Lacy stated, "He said they did bring him to that place, and when he arrived there they threw a rope around his neck. He said the rope was then thrown around the top of a telegraph pole and he said the Mexican Vega was drawn up. Disremember whether he was drawn up more times than one or not, but he was let down in a few seconds and after Vega came to his senses from being hung they questioned him." Lacy said his impression from the conversation was that Vega was pulled up by the rope multiple times before confessing. Lacy testified,

> He said that when they interrogated him till they were satisfied, he said he seen that there was a disposition in men present to take his life, which he, McMains, was opposed to. He said that he talked to bystanders . . . to use their influence to keep him from being killed. He said he seen and became satisfied that they had so much whisky that he could not avail anything with them, and he with others turned and went away, and he said Vega was killed. He said he thought they destroyed the testimony they wanted to get when he was killed.[6]

After one more witness, the defense began their case by calling Simeon Erastus Welding. After a brief introduction, Welding stated that McMains was boarding with him and that William Low was also staying in his home at the time of Vega's murder. He said both Low and McMains told him about the interrogation of Cruz Vega and added that Low expected part of the reward for finding Tolby's killers. Welding said of Low, "I heard him say something in regard to a reward offered for the murderer of Tolby. He asked me a time or two if I thought Mr. McMains received any reward, if he would receive any of it. He stated that he expected to receive some part of it." On the night of the murder, both McMains and Low were at Welding's house, located "about one-hundred yards above the Ponil bridge on the south side of the river," when gunshots rang out. He said that these shots were fired between nine and ten o'clock. Welding remembered, "It was about from half an hour to an hour after McMains came to my house that I heard the shots. He and Low returned very near the same time. Mr. McMains returned first."[7]

On cross-examination Welding was asked how he knew McMains was in his house at the time that he heard the shots. Welding responded, "I suppose he was in bed from the fact of his pulling off his boots and throwing them on the floor and making the same noise that anybody does in getting into bed. . . . The partition in the room was a wagon sheet and we could see his shadow in the room and hear him talking in the room." Welding recalled the reaction of McMains to hearing the gunfire: "He was talking to me and my wife at the time I heard the shots. He made a remark about it. He either made the remark this way, 'My God! I fear those are the shots that killed Cruz Vega.' He either used the words 'my God,' or he left it out altogether."[8]

The two days of testimony concluded Thursday evening and the case went to the jury. They returned the next afternoon with a verdict of "guilty in the fifth degree," which meant that McMains's actions and subsequent negligence led to Vega's murder. McMains was fined three hundred dollars.[9] Because the verdict did not specify what McMains was guilty of (the word "murder" was left out of the verdict), his attorneys were able to have it thrown out. A new trial was set for the spring of 1878 in Taos. At that time the charges were dismissed by Judge Samuel Parks.[10]

Shortly after the guilty in the fifth-degree verdict, Colfax County elected a new sheriff, Pete Burleson.[11] That same month, on September 26, William Morley, while working in Colorado, wrote to his wife about a business

William Raymond Morley. Under pressure from his wife to have his photo taken, Morley sat for this photo as a joke after returning from surveying work. Date and photographer unknown. Norman Cleaveland Papers, Image #00250003, Rio Grande Historical Collections, New Mexico State University Archives and Special Collections, Las Cruces, NM.

proposition McMains had made, his mother-in-law's efforts to bring light to the corruption in New Mexico, and other personal matters. Morley wrote,

My Dear One —

I have received nine letters from you since writing but you will not blame me I know for I have been almost constantly either in the saddle or on the line from morning at sunrise until dark. . . . I am rushing things as fast as possible so I can get to New Mexico and wife and babies.

After telling his wife about a painful tooth he had filled, and inviting her to camp when they were to be near Cimarron, Morley moved on to McMains:

> As to McMains' proposition. It is impossible for me to buy cattle as I have no money to buy with—to do any good. I would be glad to help Mc in any way, but this fight has cost me a good deal and I have but little money as you know and should not like to run in debt. Between ourselves I do not think he is adapted to it and has no experience. But I don't like to advise him.

Turning to his mother-in-law, Morley wrote, "The fact is she is desperately ambitious and is determined to have her own way let what will happen to us, and I propose not to be sacrificed." He continued,

> She writes me also, holding out hopes one day and dealing in threats the next. . . . I have lost faith in her ability to do much else than quarrel with those who disagree with her. She will quarrel with us sooner or later, and it might as well begin. The sooner begun the sooner ended. . . .
> Love to the babies and I would write more if I had time.
> Lovingly and faithfully,
> Raymond[12]

On November 21 William B. Matchett wrote to William Morley not only to update him on the case against Axtell but also to let him know that an unnamed person was searching for his (Morley's) affidavit (there wasn't actually an affidavit from Morley at that time). As to the identity of the person interested in Morley's statement, Matchett wrote, "I presume Elkins, for he has looked darkly at me as he has lately passed me." Of the charges against Axtell, Matchett wrote, "The affidavits are considered as settling the case as the objection here seemed to be not that the facts did not exist but that there was not a single oath to anything, while Axtell and others had sworn."[13]

While Mary McPherson had yet to accomplish her goal of getting an investigation started, she did bring the concerns of many New Mexico citizens to the attention of high-ranking government officials. Coming violence in the territory would force them to act.

Chapter 12

Axtell's "Dear Ben" Letter

The people of Colfax County received their first victory on January 14 of the new year, 1878, when the New Mexico Legislative Assembly voted to restore the courts in Colfax County.[1] Citizens of Colfax would no longer have to endure the long journey to Taos to attend court. The hard work was beginning to pay off.

While things were calming in Colfax County, Governor Samuel B. Axtell was dealing with a new outbreak of violence and lawlessness as the result of a murder in Lincoln County. On February 18, 1878, an Englishman named John Tunstall was murdered by a posse sent out by Lincoln County sheriff William Brady. The posse's purpose was to attach Tunstall's cattle for a legal case against Tunstall's business partner, Alexander McSween. Along with known outlaws, the posse was comprised of allies of the business partnership of James Dolan, whose monopoly in Lincoln County Tunstall and McSween threatened. When the posse reached Tunstall, he was gunned down in cold blood.

Following Tunstall's murder, because Sheriff Brady refused to arrest anyone with the posse that murdered Tunstall, Justice of the Peace John B. Wilson appointed Tunstall's former foreman, Richard "Dick" Brewer, a deputy constable and gave him warrants to arrest men implicated in the murder. Brewer, in turn, deputized a group of Tunstall's former employees. The young men, calling themselves the Regulators, soon arrested William Morton and Frank Baker. On their way back to the town of Lincoln (the seat of Lincoln County), Morton and Baker were killed, either gunned down by the Regulators while trying to escape or executed by them to prevent their release by Sheriff Brady.

Governor Axtell, under the influence of Thomas B. Catron, who owned a mortgage on all of Dolan's business interests, sided firmly with the Dolan faction. On March 9, the same day the Regulators would kill Morton and Baker, Axtell visited Lincoln. The Governor refused to meet with anyone sympathetic to the McSween-Tunstall side, and, upon leaving, he issued a proclamation declaring that the appointment of Justice of the Peace Wilson was illegal. By doing this he invalidated the warrants Wilson had issued and the legal authority bestowed upon the Regulators. This move left no doubt that he intended to fully support Dolan's interests. Axtell's actions turned Lincoln County into a war zone, with Tunstall allies on one side and those aligned with Tunstall's former business competitor, James J. Dolan, on the other.[2] Complaints from Lincoln County to the federal government about Axtell's actions went as high as President Hayes.[3] For Axtell this would be followed by more personal difficulty as the result of actions taken dealing with the Colfax County troubles.

Back in 1876 it was said that Axtell was going to meet with a group of Cimarron citizens, but at the last moment those citizens were warned that the meeting was some sort of trap and therefore did not show. About April 1878 a letter from Axtell to Benjamin Stevens that explained the trap came into the possession of Frank Springer. The letter was the same one that William Morley had learned of in 1876 that resulted in him and the others not showing up for the governor's expected arrival. How Springer obtained the letter is not known; however, it likely was tied to the April death of Benjamin Stevens. One possibility is that the sick Stevens, knowing he would soon die, turned the letter over to Springer or Morley, or someone else who passed it to them. Another possibility has to do with a trunk belonging to Thomas Catron that was lost (or stolen). Catron had been in Cimarron just before the death of

Stevens, and it is possible that he had taken possession of some of Stevens's files, including the letter, while there. The trunk, said by Catron to have been lost somewhere between Cimarron and Las Vegas, could have been taken off the stage by someone at Cimarron.[4]

The letter from Axtell to Stevens read,

> Dear Ben,
>
> The second telegram delivered to you at Fort Union, directed to Cimarron, was intended to leak, but the operator here says he cannot raise the Cimarron office. If I was expected, our friends would probably be on hand, as the guard is only a government escort. I do not think your definite business is suspected. Wade informed Hatch that he had been ready all the time to assist you, but could not find that you wanted to do it. Hatch says their opinion is that you weakened and do not want to arrest the man. Have your men placed to arrest him and to kill all the men who resist you or stand with those who do resist you. Our man signed the invitation with others who were at that meeting for me to visit Colfax—Porter, Morley, Springer, *et al*. Now, if they expect me Saturday they will be on hand. Send me letters by messenger, and do not hesitate at extreme measures. Your honor is at stake now, and a failure is fatal. If others resist or attempt murder, bring them also. Hatch is excited, and wishes, of course, to put all the blame on the civil officers. I am more anxious on your account than for any other reason. I clearly see that we have no friends in Colfax, and I have suspected all along that some of our pretended friends here were traitors.
>
> Yours, etc.
>
> S. B. Axtell[5]

"Our man" referred to in the letter was Clay Allison. So we have a letter where Axtell stated his desire to arrest Allison, mentioned some of his other critics by name, and wrote that he expected them all to be in the same location for a planned meeting with him. All along Axtell had no intention of going to Cimarron but only said he would to achieve another goal. Was this goal the arrest of Clay Allison or something more? Allison, who had no warrant out for his arrest, was not in hiding. Finding him would not have been difficult, as proven by his peaceful arrest (followed by a quick release) shortly after the failed trap. This suggests the goal was something more than a simple arrest. The lines of the letter that received the most attention were, "Have your men placed to arrest him and to kill all the men who resist you or stand with those who do resist you" and "do not hesitate at extreme measures." If Allison had come to meet with the governor and instead found himself confronted by soldiers, it seems likely that he would have been suspicious of their motives, which could easily have led to him resisting any effort to arrest him. This surely occurred to Axtell, and yet he called for "extreme measures" and for soldiers "to kill all the men who resist . . . or stand with those who do resist."

On April 4, Frank Springer wrote to Axtell about the letter. After summarizing it and the events of March 1876, Springer turned his attention to the governor:

> I find it impossible to put any other construction upon the language employed by you, than that you expected and desired that one result of the mission of soldiers to Cimarron, under the direction of Ben Stevens, would be the death of myself and the other persons named, and that the offense for which we were thus doomed to assassination was our having signed, as citizens of Colfax County, a courteous invitation to the Executive of the Territory to visit the county and see for himself the true state of affairs. . . .
>
> Now, as one of the persons thus singled out, and one who had never injured you, I write this to ask, what reason you, as Governor of a Territory, had for laying such a plan as this, and why you desired my destruction.
>
> I am, Sir, very respectfully
Frank Springer.[6]

Axtell replied on April 7, saying there was "some very grave mistake in this whole matter" and completely denying any attempt to injure Springer, Henry Porter, or William Morley. Axtell wrote that "Troops were asked in Colfax simply to assist the civil authorities in making arrests, not for any other purpose."[7]

Springer, not believing Axtell's denials, wrote back on the ninth, "I still fail to see why, if you had nothing against us, you should use the names of myself and the other parties mentioned, in such a significant manner, in connection with suggestions to kill not only those who resist, but the bystanders." Springer closed the letter, "Of course the letters were not intended like the telegram, for the eyes of those mentioned, but greater security would have been ensured by limiting the size of your agent[']s liquor rations."[8]

In his response on April 11, Axtell asked Springer to "please send me full copy of such letters purporting to be mine as you have in your possession and I will then be enabled to determine whether or not they are genuine, and to make such explanations, if any, as they seem to demand."[9] Springer sent the copies to Axtell a week later.[10]

Axtell didn't respond until May 13, by which time the "Dear Ben" letter had become public.[11] Axtell said his delayed reply was due to him being away from Santa Fe. He did not deny that he had written the letter they had been debating, but instead attempted to explain the letter as follows: "Uncle Ben [Stevens] had an especial warrant issued by Judge Waldo to arrest a noted desperado. I had obtained the assistance of troops for that single purpose. It was only intended to use troops to enforce the service of that writ. The sheriff of the county having advised me that he could not serve process. It was not intended to injure any one unless they resisted this lawful authority. I regret that any ambiguity in my letter should have led you to believe that violence was intended toward yourself or any other peaceable citizen."[12] Before Axtell wrote this last response to Springer, on April 18, the *Cimarron News and Press* ran the letter and story behind it.[13]

On May 23 the *News and Press* again printed the letter under the headline "A Villainous Plot." Accompanying the letter was a scathing commentary, likely written by Springer. Following a recap of events leading up the invitation for Axtell to visit Cimarron, the commentary turned to the assassination plot— as Frank Springer saw it—laid out in the letter. After the plot failed, "Ben. Stevens and his soldiers did nothing except to march out into the country to arrest one man [Clay Allison], who came in quietly with the officers and was liberated the same day; and as the Governor afterwards, while passing rapidly through the county in the coach, met this man . . . and rode with him in a friendly way some fifty miles, it is fair to presume that *he* had done nothing for which the military ought to be called out."[14]

On June 10 Springer sent affidavits that he and Morley swore out to Secretary of the Interior Carl Schurz. Springer and Morley's affidavits mostly dealt with the failed attempts to convince Axtell to visit Colfax County and

the controversy surrounding the "Dear Ben" letter. Copies of Springer's correspondence with Axtell were included. In his letter to Schurz, Springer opined,
"As one whose life was jeopardized by the actions of Mr Axtell, whether
through malevolence, stupidity, or blind partizanship [*sic*] matters little."[15]

In early July Frank Springer's father, Francis, who was well-connected
politically in Iowa, left that state with letters of introduction to Carl Schurz
and President Hayes. Francis Springer had been a delegate to the first
national convention of the Republican Party over two decades earlier and,
hoping he could influence the Republican administration of Hayes, went
to Washington to lobby for Samuel Axtell's removal as governor of New
Mexico.[16] With the "Dear Ben" letter's discovery following the outbreak of
violence in Lincoln County, the federal government could no longer ignore
the troubles in New Mexico.

Chapter 13

Frank Warner Angel

The federal government responded to the troubles in New Mexico by sending 32-year-old investigator Frank Warner Angel to the territory. Angel was born in Watertown, New York, on May 28, 1845. He graduated from the College of the City of New York (now the City College of New York) with a bachelor of arts degree in 1868. He studied law and was admitted to the New York State Bar in 1869. Angel lived and worked in Brooklyn, New York, had been married for three years, and had one daughter when he left for the territory of New Mexico.[1]

Angel was appointed special investigator representing both the Department of Justice and the Department of the Interior on April 15 and was sent to New Mexico to investigate the death of John H. Tunstall and Lincoln County violence, the charges against Governor Samuel B. Axtell and troubles in Colfax County, the alleged fraud surrounding the Uña de Gato grant, and allegations of corruption against Indian Agents Benjamin M. Thomas and Frederick C. Godfroy. Another agent, Inspector of Indian Affairs Erwin Curtis Watkins, also investigated Godfroy's actions as agent for the Mescalero Apache Indian Agency. Another of Frank Angel's directives may have been to investigate allegations of corruption or other illegal activity against United

Frank Warner Angel, graduation photo, 1868. Archives of the City College of
New York. City University of New York, NY.

States attorney Thomas B. Catron. Angel did submit a list of charges against
Catron, but those charges, as well as the affidavits supporting them, have
never been found. Frank Angel arrived in Santa Fe about two weeks after his
appointment and checked in at the Exchange Hotel.[2]

Lincoln, New Mexico, 1904. Photograph by Emerson Hough. State Historical Society of Iowa, Des Moines, IA.

In Santa Fe Angel met with Axtell, Catron, and others. He left Santa Fe for Lincoln on May 10, 1878.[3] In Lincoln County Angel took affidavits from several citizens involved on both sides of that conflict. Regarding Axtell, the statements showed that he only met with those connected to the Dolan side of the conflict and took actions to advance their interests. After Frank Angel had completed his investigation in Lincoln County, he returned to Santa Fe to await funds to investigate in Colfax County.[4]

With the investigation ongoing and Lincoln County having turned into a war zone, Governor Axtell inexplicably decided it was a good time to take a vacation. On July 17 Axtell wrote to President Hayes requesting a ninety-day leave of absence to visit family in Ohio.[5] He'd still be awaiting an answer as Angel's investigation played out to conclusion.

While Angel was in Santa Fe, the unrest in Lincoln County led to a five-day battle in the town of Lincoln that culminated with the burning of the home of Alexander McSween. Five men, including McSween, died as a young man known as William H. Bonney led a nighttime escape from the burning home.[6] Bonney would go on to gain international fame as Billy the Kid.

When Frank Warner Angel went to Cimarron in August, he may have already had copies of the affidavits sworn to by local citizens in 1877. He included these affidavits in his final report, and his questions show he knew a great deal about the situation. He did not interview William Morley, who was working for the New Mexico and Southern Pacific Railroad and not in the area at this time, though Morley did make sworn statements in May and June that might have been intended for Angel.[7] Frank Angel only included one deposition done in Cimarron in his report—that of Frank Springer. On August 9 Angel interviewed Springer with notary public Harry Whigham as witness.[8]

Angel's first question to Springer was, "What is your name and occupation?"

Springer answered, "My name is Frank Springer and I am, by profession, an attorney at law."

"What do you know about troubles in Colfax County? When and how did they originate, and what was their character? State fully all you know."

Springer began by telling what he knew about the dispute between the Maxwell Land Grant and Railway Company and settlers before his arrival in 1873 and what he had heard about "a so-called 'Ring.'"

Angel said, "You have spoken of a 'Ring.' What do you know of its existence?"

Springer stated, "The facts upon which its existence was predicated were not generally within my personal knowledge, except as to facts connected with subsequent troubles in Colfax County which impressed me with the belief that a few men had almost absolute control of affairs in this territory. In 1873, Mr. M. W. Mills, who had been a prominent opponent of the Maxwell Company, and of the men who controlled it, was elected a member of the territorial legislature. Very soon after this he became very intimate with Dr. Longwill whom he had before strongly opposed and after he went to Santa Fe to attend the session of the legislature, he wrote to Longwill in which he informed him that 'by a little sharp figuring' he had 'got in

Frank Springer. Photograph by Albright Art Parlors, date unknown. Negative #011026, Palace of the Governors Photo Archives, Santa Fe, NM (NMHM/DCA).

with the big side.'" A copy of the letter accompanied the statement. How Springer obtained it wasn't reported. He continued, "From that time on Mills became and continued very intimate with Longwill, as well as with Messer Elkins and Catron and represented them in business and political matters in the county to a large extent . . . in 1875, when Mills was again a candidate for the legislature and Longwill for Probate Judge, all their powers were exerted to promote his election. A circumstance came under my observation during that election campaign which impressed this strongly on my mind. In June [actually May 30], 1875, a man by the name of Francisco Griego murdered two soldiers in Cimarron in a gaming table quarrel. . . . He fled and was a fugitive for some time when at last he came in and gave himself up. He was at once taken before the Justice of the Peace who was a clerk in Mills' office and examined and bound over to await the action of the Grand Jury on $1,000 bail, this action of the justice being taken after an hour recess and a consultation with Longwill and Mills, as I was audibly informed at the time by several persons. The political campaign was then opening, and some weeks afterward I had a conversation with one C. Lara, an especial friend of Griego, who was then actively working in the interest of the Longwill and Mills ticket, as was also Griego himself. Lara had previously been on the other side and in my asking him the reason of his change of attitude he told me that his friend was in danger of prosecution for the killing of the soldiers, and that he, Lara, had been to Santa Fe, and had talked with the gentlemen, and that they had promised him that if he and Griego would use all their influence with the Mexicans in favor of the ticket of Elkins and Longwill, his friend Griego should not suffer. . . . Upon my asking him who the gentlemen were who had promised this, he mentioned, with much reluctance, Messrs. Breeden and Catron. Whether his statement was true or not I do not know, but I observed that both Lara and Griego labored earnestly in the direction indicated, and that when the District Court came in in September, Lara was appointed interpreter for the Grand Jury, and although the most positive and abundant evidence was produced against him, Griego was discharged without being indicted for anything, nor were any further proceedings taken against him in the matter."

Angel asked, "What was the cause of the troubles in Colfax County since you lived there?"

"The assassination of Reverend F. J. Tolby in September, 1875."

"State the circumstances connected with the death of Tolby and what followed. State all you know about it."

"F. J. Tolby was a minister of the Methodist church who had been stationed in Cimarron and had been doing missionary work in the county for nearly two years. He was a man of ability and rather free in talking about men and their acts. During the first week in September, 1875, while the court was in session at Cimarron, Judge Palen and Tolby had a rather spirited altercation, the judge denouncing him for some remarks he had made about the court and its actions. Tolby immediately declared he would write up that judge so that two-hundred thousand readers should see his record, which led some to suppose that he might have been the author of some letters which had appeared in the eastern press reflecting on Palen, Elkins, and others."[9]

Springer told Angel of the assassination of Tolby. He described the fates of accused assassins Cruz Vega and Manuel Cardenas, their accusations against Robert Longwill, Melvin Mills, and Florencio Donoghue, and the events that immediately followed. Springer was then questioned about and described Axtell's actions in response to the Colfax County troubles.

"Was it necessary to attach Colfax to Taos County for judicial purposes?" Angel asked.

"No. Not for any legitimate end," Springer opined.

"What was the object of attaching Colfax County to Taos?"

"The alleged reason was that lawlessness prevailed in Colfax and the laws could not be enforced, but it was not true," Springer claimed. "There was no resistance or defiance of law, save in these isolated instances which occur in all communities and which the great body of the people were willing and ready to suppress and punish whenever the machinery of justice was put in motion to that end. There was no more crime in the county than in other counties throughout the territory, nor than there had been in previous years in Colfax County. . . . In past years there had been a great failure of justice in Colfax County, but it was not the fault of the people of the county generally, but was due to the fact that those who controlled the prosecuting of offenders, through selection of juries, et cetera, prevented prosecutions, as in the case of Griego above mentioned. Repeated continuances of cases, acquittals, and discharges of known murderers had shaken faith in the administration of the law, and of this none complained more bitterly than the people of Colfax County themselves. In my opinion, judging by what occurred subsequently, as well as at the time, the real object of the annexation of Colfax County to Taos was to so intimidate and punish, by means of indictments . . . the people who had taken an active part in the search for the Tolby murderers, and who had become thoroughly hostile to the suspected parties, and thus enable these parties to require control in the county which through these events they had lost."[10]

Angel questioned Springer more on the attachment of Colfax County to Taos for judicial purposes, about what the people of Colfax did to stop it, and how Axtell responded to their pleas. In answer to one of Angel's questions, Springer brought up the "Dear Ben" letter. Springer went into great detail about the alleged plot. Angel followed that with a question about the indictment of Ada Morley for taking a letter from the post office. Springer blamed the Santa Fe Ring and said when he asked Longwill to use his influence to have the indictment dismissed, Longwill told him that William "Morley ought to stop attacking Elkins through the newspaper." After one more general question about the corruption in New Mexico, the interview ended.[11]

Angel left the meeting with copies of the "Dear Ben" letter and Springer's correspondence with Axtell about it.[12] What Angel learned from Springer seems to have changed his view on Axtell. While there may have been other factors, such as the escalation of violence in Lincoln County, it appears Angel left Colfax County with a much more negative view of the governor than he had after visiting Lincoln County. Angel immediately returned to Santa Fe, intent on making Axtell answer for his actions.

Angel sent Axtell the charges made against him and requested an immediate reply. The following day, Monday, August 12, a defiant Axtell sent his reply. He began, "You furnish me with a list of 31 interrogations which imply about as many charges of corrupt misconduct in my office and ask that I should reply to them in 24 hours. Do you think this reasonable?" The governor addressed two of the charges, asking who made them and if the statements against him were made under oath. Then he turned his attention to the investigator, saying that after Angel returned to Santa Fe from Lincoln, he told him "that there was not the scratch of a pen against" him. Governor Axtell asked, "Under what influences has this cross sprung up so suddenly?" Of course, the answer was that what Angel learned in Colfax County caused him to reexamine all the evidence. Axtell promised to answer the charges once they were "completed," and, in closing, wrote to Angel, "If you choose to stand as my accuser well and good, if not then give me the name or names of the parties who make these charges. I am anxious to do right and I have been taught that a part of doing right is not to submit to a wrong."[13]

That same day Axtell wrote to Collis Potter Huntington, asking his friend to use his influence to have Secretary of State William M. Evarts change Angel's report before it was submitted to the Interior Department.[14] Angel replied to Axtell's letter of August 12 the following day and explained his position:

> I have found certain parts of this Territory in a terrible and deplorable state—some one is responsible for the same, and with a view to try and discover if you were responsible for the same I prepared and forwarded the interrogatories to you without the least personal feeling against you but on the contrary with the greatest esteem and regard for you, which interrogatories are based on correspondence and papers in the Departments and representations made to me in conversation with various citizens substantiated (without your reply) in part by affidavit of Frank Springer the original of which I submitted to you yesterday. I enclose all papers which I have (as per paper enclosed marked A)— most of which I believe you have already received from the Department—which either reflect directly or indirectly on you and desire a full and complete answer thereto. . . .
>
> You desire to know if I had given you a reasonable time to reply to said interrogatories. I can only say that if I was the accused party I should not want desire or wish twenty four hours to answer same.

Angel gave Axtell thirty days to reply, but added that the thirty days was subject to the approval of Secretary of the Interior Carl Schurz.[15] Frank Angel then returned to New York City and on August 24 he wrote to Schurz, sent Schurz copies of his correspondence with Axtell, and closed, "I have given him thirty days to reply subject to *your approval*."[16]

Angel followed the letter with a verbal report to Schurz. Schurz said of the report, in a letter to President Hayes, "After listening to Mr. Angells [*sic*] verbal report, it became clear to my mind that we ought to make a change in the Governorship of N.M. the sooner the better, and as Genl. Wallace has indicated his willingness to serve, we ought to have him on the spot as speedily as possible. It is also desirable that Genl. Wallace should come here before going to his post, in order to receive all the information Mr. Angells [*sic*] can give him, so as to be well posted and to avoid mistakes in the beginning."[17]

Chapter 14

A Change in Governorship

Though Frank Angel's report hadn't been completed yet, Samuel B. Axtell was suspended as the governor of the territory of New Mexico on September 4, 1878. The suspension was actually a permanent removal. Axtell was immediately replaced by Lew Wallace.[1] Word of the removal reached Frank Springer and others in Cimarron about a week before it was announced. Springer waited for the official announcement before reporting in the *News and Press* "that Gov. Axtell's official head was . . . to be lopped off." Springer, the only editor of the paper in town at the time, used the *News and Press* to celebrate. Under the headlines "The Bishop Boosted" and "Axtell's Head Falls at Last," Springer wrote,

> The reception of this news created more enthusiasm in Cimarron than anything since the restoration of our courts. The exultation of victory, well earned after a long fight, took possession of our people, and general joy and congratulation prevailed. This feeling soon took shape in active demonstrations. Powder was offered on every hand, and a pair of heavy anvils, managed by experienced hands, served as an implement for saluting purposes, fully equal to a 12-lb cannon. A parting salute of fifty guns was given in honor of the decapitation of El Obispo. . . .

The firing was heard by the ranch men, some of whom rigged up
an anvil and answered gun for gun. . . .
"I see clearly that we have no friends in Colfax."—*Axtell*.
Right, old boy, for once.[2]

William Morley and O. P. McMains both happened to be in Tucson at the same
time when they received the news of Axtell's removal in a telegram from Ada
Morley. Morley replied to his wife, "I just wanted to go out in the street and throw
up my hat and howl . . . we [Morley, McMains, and another man] all wished so
much that we could be in Cimarron and help fire the anvil and celebrate."[3]

Taking the opposite view of the *News and Press*, the *Santa Fe New
Mexican* defended Axtell in multiple editorials, including a September
commentary that read in part, "A Mr. Frank W. Angell [*sic*] of New York City
has been conducting a curious sort of an 'investigation' of Governor S. B.
Axtell of New Mexico, under a commission from the President and Secretary
Schurz. From the tenor of reports in the Santa Fe papers, he appears to have
gone round the Territory picking up all the gossip and slander of sore-heads
and removed officials, which he finally embodied in a bill of indictment, as it
were, against Governor Axtell, consisting of thirty-one questions."[4]

Axtell denied the allegations publicly and then, instead of writing to
Angel, wrote to the *Santa Fe New Mexican* and sent a newspaper clipping of
his denials as his official response.[5] Privately, a livid Axtell tore into Angel
and his investigation in a letter to Collis Huntington. Axtell questioned
whether it was still possible to "undo any of Angel's evil work," then turned
his attention to the investigator, writing, "I know him to be a dirty slanderous
liar, and I am not willing to allow his accusations to pass uncontradicted."
About his quick removal, Axtell vented, "They did not even have the grace to
wait thirty—no not ten days to receive my answer—but threw me over-board
without a chance even to reply to his dirty insinuations!"[6]

Axtell would not be able to undo Angel's work. He was done as the
governor of the territory, which is not surprising considering Angel's reports,
the numerous affidavits that supported the charges, and the ongoing lawlessness
that continued in Lincoln County. Frank W. Angel completed his report and
submitted it to Secretary of the Interior Carl Schurz on October 3, 1878. Angel
began by saying that he believed Axtell's removal as governor was in "the

Samuel B. Axtell. Date and photographer unknown. MWDL Record #237286, used by permission, Classified Photo Collection, Utah State Historical Society, Millcreek, UT.

best interests of New Mexico." Angel commented on the obstruction he faced during his investigation: "*I* was met by every opposition possible by the United States civil officials and every obstacle thrown in my way by them to prevent a full and complete examination—with one exception and that of the surveyor general who not only sought but insisted on a full and thorough examination as will more fully appear by my report submitted as to his office."[7]

Angel listed twelve charges made against Samuel Axtell. Following the charges he wrote that Axtell tried to "ignore the complaints against him on the ground that the Department of the Interior had no power to investigate him." When Axtell did finally reply to the charges, he did so not by sworn statement, Angel complained, but by sending an unsigned newspaper clipping. Of the governor Angel wrote, "He is a man of strong prejudices, impulsive, conceited and easily flattered—all these make a man easily influenced[—]a complete tool in the hands of designing men."[8]

Angel moved on to the results of his investigation. The first eight charges related to affairs in Lincoln County. Of these charges Angel found enough evidence to conclude that the following six charges were sustained: (1) that the governor had taken strictly partisan action as to the troubles in Lincoln County; (2) that he refused to listen to the complaints of the people of that county; (3) that he arbitrarily removed territorial officers, thereby outlawing citizens and usurping the functions of the judiciary; (4) that he removed officials and in their place appointed strong partisans; (5) that all action taken by him has increased rather than quieted the troubles in Lincoln County; and (6) that he appointed officials to office and kept them there who were supported by the worst outlaws and murderers that the territory could produce. Another charge, that he knowingly appointed bad men to office, involved two appointments. Angel found the charge sustained on one of the two cases. As to the ninth charge, "*That* he was a tool of designing men[—]Weak and arbitrary in exercising the functions of his office," Angel simply wrote, "I find [this charge] has been sustained as appears from facts set forth herein." Here Angel felt that the evidence put forth in charges one through eight was enough to sustain the charge as he provided no further explanation. Had he felt the need to, he could have given evidence as to Axtell's handling of the troubles in Colfax County to further support the charge. Regarding the tenth charge ("*That* he was a mormon and desired to turn the Territory into a mormon settlement"), Frank Angel reported that there was no evidence to support the allegation.[9]

The eleventh charge against Axtell was "*That* he conspired to murder innocent and law abiding citizens because they opposed his wishes and were exerting their influence against him." In his report Angel described the bill attaching Colfax County to Taos for judicial purposes and told how Axtell

refused requests by Colfax County citizens to meet with them before signing
the bill. Angel wrote that, at the time the bill was passed, the troubles in the
county had stopped "and that there was more lawlessness in other parts of
the Territory than in Colfax." Angel further stated that nothing was accomplished by the law, and that "it was a gross injury and injustice to the people
of Colfax County," saying that "the two counties are separated by a range
of high mountains . . . which when the court is in session are difficult and
dangerous to cross," and adding, "The juries were entirely taken from Taos
County, manipulated by Pedro Sanches[,] a ringite, and prejudiced by out
side influence."[10]

Angel reported that, after Axtell's initial refusals to meet with the people
of Colfax, a letter, "signed by ten or twelve prominent citizens" was sent to
Axtell "inviting him to visit Colfax County and make a thorough investigation and learn the facts for himself." Axtell made no reply. Shortly after,
Benjamin Stevens shared the telegram from Axtell claiming he was going
to visit Cimarron. Angel wrote that Axtell "did not intend to visit Colfax
Co. and that the action of Stevens was in furtherance of a plot as will appear
by the following letter." Here, Angel included a newspaper clipping of the
"Dear Ben" letter. Angel's report continued,

> Was there ever a cooler devised plot with a Govenor [*sic*] as sponsor?
> The Govenor [*sic*] admits the letter in toto . . . "That it sounds like
> me" . . . and then subsequently attempts to explain away part of its
> terrible features. . . .
> He makes no attempt as to the telegram. Nor why he wished it to
> "*leak*" But by a down right falsehood he attempts to assemble certain
> persons who are obnoxious to him so that in the event of the resistance,
> to be arrested, of a person by the name of Allison an excuse would be
> offered "*to kill all the men who resist or stand with those who resist
> you*".
> *He* does not explain this he cannot.
> *Stevens* and the soldiers were sent by Govenor Axtel [*sic*] osten-
> sibly to arrest a person by the name of Allison—but reading the fore-
> going telegram and letter I do not believe that it was the real object,
> for Allison was afterwards arrested and at once set at liberty . . . and
> Govenor Axtel [*sic*] subsequently made an appointment and traveled
> with said Allison in a friendly way in the stage coach. . . .

Any man capable of framing and trying to enforce such a letter of instructions as the one set forth in this report is not fit to be entrusted with any power whatever. I therefore report that this charge has been sustained.

As to the next charge, "*That* he arbitrarily refused to restore the courts to Colfax County and refused to listen to the petitions of the people of that County for the restoration thereof," Angel concluded, "For the reasons set forth under charge Eleventh I find that this charge is sustained." Angel closed,

> *In conclusion* I respectfully submit that whether through ignorance or corrupt motives the action of said Axtel [*sic*] has been to keep many parts of the Territory of New Mexico in a state of termoil [*sic*] and confusion, when intelligent and non-partizan [*sic*] action on his part might have avoided much of the difficulty, and that the removal of Govenor Axtel [*sic*] viewed with the evidence and his reply received before my first report, was an absolute necessity, and it becomes still more evident that such was the right course on receiving his subsequent replies.
>
> *It is* seldom that history states more corruption, fraud, mismanagement, plots and murders, than New Mexico, has been the theatre under the administration of Govenor Axtel [*sic*].[11]

Of the twelve charges against Samuel Axtell, none was more serious than the alleged plot laid out in the "Dear Ben" letter. The question remains, Was Axtell's intention to have innocent citizens murdered, or did he simply choose poor wording when writing the letter? Frank Springer took the position that Axtell's motive was unimportant when he wrote, "As one whose life was jeopardized by the actions of Mr Axtell, whether through malevolence, stupidity, or blind partizanship [*sic*] matters little."[12] While this may be true, Axtell's motive must be addressed. It seems difficult to believe that when Axtell wrote, "Have your men placed to arrest him and to kill all the men who resist you or stand with those who do resist you," and added, "do not hesitate at extreme measures," he did not realize the potential consequences of these orders.

If Axtell did want the men named in the letter dead, the questions are, Why, and was it his idea? The men expected at the meeting had all been outspoken critics of the governor and other New Mexico politicians associated with what is known as the Santa Fe Ring. They were also interested in seeing whoever might be behind the assassination of Reverend Tolby brought to justice. Did Axtell want to silence troublesome critics who, for the most part, he did not even know? Or was he pushed by political allies who worried that the murder of Tolby would come back to them? Did Donoghue, Mills, and Longwill pay to have Tolby assassinated? If so, did they come up with the plan, or were they acting at someone else's behest? Was it them or someone else who came up with the plot described in Axtell's letter? The evidence does not exist to answer these questions definitively.

Frank Angel's charge that Axtell "was a tool of designing men" may well be the case. Axtell had only been the governor of New Mexico for a couple of months when the Colfax troubles broke out. It was early the next year when he wrote the letter to Ben Stevens. It seems unlikely that he would, on his own, desire the extermination of so many citizens after such a limited time in the territory. However, this was the same man who referred to those who opposed his signing of one bill as "traitors," so it was enough time for Axtell, whether on his own or under the influence of others, to develop a very negative opinion of certain parties. Whatever his reasons or who was behind the "Dear Ben" plot, Axtell's handling of the troubles in Lincoln County and his repeated dismissals of those in Colfax County clearly demonstrated his willingness to listen to only one side of a conflict before taking decisive action. In taking that approach he exacerbated both the Colfax and Lincoln County Wars.

Lew Wallace replaced Axtell as governor of the territory of New Mexico. The 51-year-old was an experienced military veteran who served in the Mexican-American War and rose to the rank of major general in the American Civil War. After the war he was a member of the court that tried those accused of having conspired to assassinate President Abraham Lincoln. Wallace was a lawyer and an author. The governorship was a position he didn't really want, but Wallace accepted it in the hopes that it would lead to an ambassadorship.[13]

Lew Wallace. Date and photographer unknown. Lew Wallace Collection,
M0292, box 24, folder 1, 1904_#1, William H. Smith Memorial Library,
Indiana Historical Society, Indianapolis, IN.

Chapter 15

End of the Colfax County War

ew Wallace traveled to Trinidad, Colorado, by railroad, and from there continued his journey to Santa Fe by stagecoach. On his way to the territorial capital, he stopped at Cimarron, where he spent a night and met with Frank Springer and others. Of the mood in Cimarron, Wallace wrote, "Without reference to the past, there certainly appears to be a good feeling on the part of the citizens there, and a decided disposition to keep the peace."[1]

Wallace arrived in Santa Fe on the night of September 29, 1878, and met with Axtell on October 1 to arrange the transfer of power.[2] In a letter to his wife, Susan, Lew Wallace went into detail about his meeting with Axtell, starting with his morning arrival at the Palace of the Governors.

> Several gentlemen were with him, some others went with me. I found him in what is called the Executive office—a large, low, dark chamber, one of many in the palace. The carpet was old and dirty. There was a large table in the center, a settee covered with stained and greasy calico, a few chairs—these constituted the furniture. On the north wall there was a great mob almost as yellow as the walls themselves. The ceiling was of dirty muslin tacked to the rafters. The only cheerful thing in the apartment was the fire blazing in the open fire-place. In every corner hung dusty cobwebs, every crack, and catch was a mass of sooty dust. No need to make comments. Such a picture of neglect and indifference you never saw as that office is.

The Governor was sitting at the table when I entered. He arose to receive me, giving me to see a good looking, gray haired, dark-eyed, pleasant featured man, about fifty-five years old, and a gentleman. As you may imagine, the interview was not a pleasant one; yet he went through it very well. After the introduction, we shook hands, and I said, "I have come to pay my respects to you, Governor, and ask when it will be agreeable to you to present my papers." He replied, "I have been expecting you, General, and of course know all about your business. It is not my pleasure that is to be consulted, but yours." "Will tomorrow suit you then?" I asked. "Certainly." I then remarked, "That off our hands, it remains to speak of the mode.["] [Axtell said, "]For my part, the most unceremonious method of transfer will be the most agreeable. I prefer it should [be] as private as possible, but down by writing, for the sake of record [for] parties in Washington who were very energetic in trying to oust me, and have themselves appointed. I also know you were not one of them; that this place was tendered you without solicitation on your part. If your coming is in the least degree a disappointment to me, it is more than counterbalanced by the fact that your appointment was a defeat to my enemies." Of course I assured the Governor that I had had nothing to do with his removal. . . .

We branched off there into a general conversation in which the whole company took part.[3]

Palace of the Governors, circa 1880. Photograph by D. B. Chase. Author's collection.

To the end Axtell was obsessed with his so-called enemies, never compre-
hending that it was not him but his actions that those who lobbied for his
removal had a problem with.

While O. P. McMains continued his fight against the land grants, for
most the removal of Samuel Axtell as governor was the end of the Colfax
County War. By meeting with the county's citizens in Cimarron, Wallace
had done something Axtell had refused to. No further effort by Wallace was
needed to keep the peace there. Still, the fact that Wallace rejected all over-
tures to connect himself with the Santa Fe Ring surely pleased the masses in
Colfax County. Of the Ring Wallace wrote, "I came here, and found a 'Ring'
with a hand on the throat of the Territory. I refused to join them, and now they
are proposing to fight me in the Senate."[4] While his refusal to join the Ring
was a commendable start to his governorship, his overall tenure as governor
resulted in much failure. The main issue Wallace had to contend with was
the violence in Lincoln County, and for too long a time he took only small,
ineffective actions that allowed the bloodshed to continue. He did more to
help quell the violence after he finally visited Lincoln County, but he seemed
more concerned with finishing his novel *Ben-Hur* than with the problems of
the territory.

After Axtell's removal as governor of New Mexico, he returned to Ohio,
moving to Richfield (north of Akron). In 1881, when rumors circulated that
Axtell was being considered for a judicial position, Republican Party leaders
in Akron wrote to President James A. Garfield that Axtell's "reputation as a
politician in this community is unsavory to the greatest degree"—and that
was from his own party. Commenting on the same rumored appointment,
a piece in an Akron newspaper opined that if Axtell was to serve in public
office, "it must come of Federal appointment, because Mr. Axtell could never
get anything by popular vote." Axtell never did receive an appointment from
President Garfield, but following Garfield's assassination, President Chester
Arthur appointed Axtell chief justice of the supreme court of New Mexico.
He served on the court from 1882 until he stepped down in 1885. Axtell
remained in New Mexico, where he practiced law and, in 1890, became
chairman of the territorial Republican committee. He died on August 6, 1891,
while visiting Morristown, New Jersey.[5]

Many will remember Samuel Beach Axtell only for his time as the governor of the territory of New Mexico and for the bloodshed in Lincoln and Colfax Counties that took place on his watch. His one-sided, partisan handling of events exacerbated both the Lincoln County War and the Colfax County War. Considering he was new to New Mexico and didn't have any past connections to the people he worked against, it seems likely the reason for Axtell's mishandling of the conflicts was that he put too much trust in the word of a few, or, as Frank Angel wrote, he was simply "a tool of designing men." Had he taken the time to listen to both sides of each conflict, rather than blindly trusting those who had his ear, some of the violence and death could have been prevented. It is for these mistakes that Axtell will be remembered.

The man whose investigation led to Axtell's removal, Frank Warner Angel, was appointed assistant United States attorney for the Eastern District of New York before the end of 1878 and later served as fire commissioner of Jersey City, New Jersey. He died in Jersey City on March 15, 1906, at the age of sixty.[6]

Fallout from Angel's investigation included Thomas Benton Catron's resignation as United States attorney. What charges he made against Catron is not known. While existing correspondence shows that Angel submitted a report and list of charges against Catron following his investigation, those charges, as well as any affidavits dealing specifically with Catron, have never been found. It is possible that Catron's good friend Steve Elkins had the Catron report destroyed. Catron was still worried that a report from Angel would be used against him in the early 1890s and wrote multiple letters to Elkins, who was then secretary of war, asking him to destroy it. In "Smooth Steve" Elkins's last reply to Catron on the subject, he claimed to have made a "diligent search" for the report but said, "it cannot be found." Was this Elkins's way of telling Catron the matter had been taken care of? Following Catron's resignation, he continued to practice law and held various public offices. He was elected to the territorial council numerous times, ran three times to be New Mexico's delegate to Congress, losing twice and winning once, and served as mayor of Santa Fe from 1906 to 1908. When New Mexico was admitted as the forty-seventh state in 1912, the New Mexico Legislature elected Catron as one of the state's two senators. Thomas B. Catron died in 1921.[7]

Frank Warner Angel, circa 1902. From the December 31, 1902, issue of the *Evening Journal* (Jersey City). New Jersey State Archives, Department of State, Trenton, NJ.

Stephen B. Elkins married Hallie Davis (his second wife; his first was deceased), daughter of a West Virginia senator, and moved to West Virginia. He cofounded the town of Elkins and later, with his father-in-law, Henry Gassaway Davis, established Davis and Elkins College. He managed the presidential campaign of Benjamin Harrison, served as Harrison's secretary of war from 1891 to 1893, and served as senator from West Virginia from 1895 until his death on January 4, 1911.[8] His 1911 death meant that good friends Elkins and Catron missed the chance to serve in the US Senate together, with Catron not getting there until a year after Elkins's death.

Both Robert Longwill and Melvin Mills, who were accused of conspiring to assassinate Reverend Tolby, had success following the Colfax County War, though Longwill's successes were cut short by an early death. Robert

Thomas B. Catron. Date and photographer unknown. Author's collection.

Longwill was director of the First National Bank of Santa Fe, married, and had young children when he died in his fifties in 1895. Melvin Whitson Mills served multiple terms in the New Mexico Legislative Assembly, served as district attorney, had a successful law practice, and had other business interests that included farming (fruit growing) and ranching. He had heavy

Stephen B. Elkins. Date and photographer unknown. Author's collection.

financial losses because of a 1904 flood, which would cause him to lose his
beloved mansion in Springer. Melvin Mills was survived by a wife and four
adopted children when he died in 1925.[9]

William Raymond Morley continued his railroad work until his accidental
death on the job when he was in Mexico studying possible train routes. He was
riding in a carriage on January 3, 1883, when a rifle accidentally discharged,

William Raymond Morley, circa 1880. Photographer unknown. Norman Cleaveland Papers, Image #00250001, Rio Grande Historical Collections, New Mexico State University Archives and Special Collections, Las Cruces, NM.

shooting him in the heart. William Morley was 36. Along with his wife, Ada, he left three children fatherless (the couple had four, but one son died in 1880). Funeral services were held in the Plaza Hotel in Las Vegas, New Mexico.[10]

His widow, Ada, remarried in 1884 to a man named Floyd Jarrett. The quick new marriage was looked upon unfavorably by many of Ray Morley's friends. The family settled on a ranch in the Datil Mountains

Ada Morley. Photograph by James N. Furlong, date unknown.
Negative #097965, Palace of the Governors Photo Archives, Santa Fe,
NM (NMHM/DCA).

in Socorro County, New Mexico. After a few years Floyd Jarrett left
Ada. The difficult life of raising three children on a secluded ranch
was compounded by financial troubles.[11] In 1897 she lost her mother,
Mary Elizabeth McPherson. McPherson, who took it upon herself to

investigate Governor Axtell's actions after Reverend Tolby's assassination, lived in Washington, DC, but was visiting Boston when she died.[12]

Ada, despite her financial difficulties, continued to lead an influential life as a writer and an active participant in many causes, such as the women's suffrage movement. Her fight to get women the right to vote once again brought her into conflict with Thomas B. Catron, who as a New Mexico senator sat on the senate committee on woman's suffrage and strongly opposed giving women the right to vote. Ada Morley organized the Society for the Prevention of Cruelty to Animals in New Mexico, the Society for the Prevention of Cruelty to Children in New Mexico, and became president of the New Mexico Chapter of the Women's Christian Temperance Union. Her eyesight failed her in her later years. Ada Morley died on December 9, 1917, at age 65, less than three years before women gained the right to vote with the ratification of the Nineteenth Amendment.[13]

Frank Springer was active in a wide variety of interests throughout his life, including a legal career, continued work for the Maxwell Land Grant and Railway Company (which would change its name to the Maxwell Land Grant Company after a reorganization in 1879), a study of paleontology that made him a renowned expert on fossil crinoids, a partnership in a cattle business with his brother Charles in what would become the CS Cattle Company, and raising a large family, though that last responsibility fell largely on his wife, Josephine, as Frank's other interests often kept him separated from his family. Springer was an invaluable asset to the Maxwell Land Grant and Railway Company, so much so that when it became clear the coming railroad would not reach Cimarron and a new town had to be formed, the company named the town Springer (to Springer's surprise). Frank Springer would eventually become president of the company.

Springer retired from legal practice in 1906 due to heart disease. He remained active in the Maxwell Land Grant Company but otherwise devoted the remainder of his life to philanthropic and scientific pursuits. The Smithsonian's Springer Collection of fossil crinoids, which he donated to the museum in 1911, is the largest fossil crinoid collection in the world. In 1924, because of health problems caused by a heart attack a year earlier, Springer moved in with his daughter, Ada, and her husband,

Frank Springer. Photograph by Kenneth Chapman, date unknown. Negative #027342, Palace of the Governors Photo Archives, Santa Fe, NM (NMHM/DCA).

Warren Davis, in Philadelphia. Frank Springer died at their home on September 22, 1927.[14]

The Maxwell Land Grant Company, which Springer devoted so much of his life to, sold off most of its American real estate in the first half of the twentieth century and sold the rest shortly thereafter. The company ended its existence in the Netherlands as De Maxwell Petroleum Holding N.V., which was bought out in 2000.[15]

The town of Cimarron never experienced the growth some expected. One reason for this was that when the railroad finally passed through Colfax County, it went through Springer, not Cimarron. The Colfax County seat was moved from Cimarron to Springer in 1881 (and moved to Raton in 1897). A railroad line did finally reach Cimarron in 1906, spurring the creation of "New Town," leaving "Old Town," which was the scene of so much excitement during the Colfax County War, to stay much as it was. Today Cimarron and the surrounding area is known for ranching, the Philmont Scout Ranch (the largest Boy Scout ranch of its kind in the world), outdoor activities such as hiking and camping, and tourism, with the Old Mill Museum and the St. James Hotel as reminders of the town's Wild West past.[16]

Robert Clay Allison, who is said to have once told Henry Lambert, "I never killed a man that didn't need killing," left his gunfighter reputation behind and settled in West Texas. In 1881 Allison married America Medora "Dora" McCulloch. Clay and Dora eventually bought a ranch near the Texas–New Mexico border. In 1885 their first daughter, Patti, was born in Colfax County, New Mexico. Two years later Allison was in Pecos, Texas, buying supplies to take back to his ranch. It was a trip he made often, but this one was to be his last. While returning to his ranch, Clay Allison fell from his wagon and was killed, probably from the wheel running over his head or neck. Clay Allison was dead at the age of 45. Seven months later his second daughter, Clay Pearl Allison, was born.[17]

Robert "Clay" and America Medora "Dora" Allison, February 1881. Wedding photo, photographer unknown. Reprint from *Clay Allison: Portrait of a Shootist* by Chuck Parsons. Permission to publish courtesy of West of the Pecos Museum, Pecos, TX

Chapter 16

O. P. McMains versus the Maxwell Land Grant

Following Axtell's removal as the governor of New Mexico, Oscar P. McMains continued his fight against the size of the Maxwell Land Grant while also facing some personal changes. He was not reappointed by the Methodist Episcopal Church to the Cimarron-Elizabethtown circuit, so McMains was back to being a traveling elder. After a brief stint in the rapidly declining town of Otero, McMains and his wife, Mary, moved to a home just south of Raton on the Red River. The land was within the Maxwell Land Grant and the Maxwell Land Grant Company expected him to purchase the property if he was going to live there, which, of course, McMains refused to do. McMains was a leader among two groups that were fighting to reduce the size of the grant—one located in Colfax County, New Mexico, and the other in Stonewall, Colorado. The groups received a defeat when, on May 19, 1879, the United States government issued a quitclaim for the grant, allowing it to be patented at over 1.7 million acres.[1] But this didn't stop the fight.

The goal of the anti-granters was not to eliminate the Maxwell Land Grant but to drastically reduce the size. One of their targets was the Elkins-Marmon survey, which they believed to be inaccurate. It was decided that an anti-grant newspaper would help the cause, so McMains, with his past newspaper experience, took control and helped establish the weekly *Raton Comet*.[2]

McMains's strong anti-grant position put him at odds with, and on the attack against, former allies and friends. Ray Morley, in a letter to his wife, wrote of McMains, "I'll tell you why I am down on him. You know what Chase and Dawson, Springer, Whigham and ourselves did for that man. He has during the last six months without cause assailed Springer and Whigham with charges of perjury and suborning of perjury, knowing at the time he was lying. This in his paper. . . . He has used his influence to persuade squatters to occupy the land owned, bought and paid for, by Springer and myself." Morley added that he did not believe the Elkins and Marmon survey was fraudulent.[3]

It wasn't long before McMains sold the *Comet*, but not because he was giving up the fight. Quite the opposite; McMains sold the paper as he prepared to travel to Washington to lobby against the grant, with money for this being provided by settlers on the grant.[4] O. P. McMains's summer in the nation's capital coincided with the assassination of President James A. Garfield, who was shot by a disgruntled office seeker at a Washington railroad station on July 2, 1881, and died on September 19.[5]

The 1881 trip McMains took was his first of many to Washington to lobby against the Maxwell Land Grant's boundaries. This first visit was to petition the government to bring a suit against the Maxwell Land Grant patent, alleging the northern boundary was inaccurate. He filed a petition on July 15, and a month later Secretary of the Interior Samuel J. Kirkwood gave his recommendation in its favor and passed the case on to the Department of Justice and Attorney General Isaac Wayne MacVeagh. Frank Springer, as attorney for the Maxwell Land Grant Company, fought against the petition. In early 1882 new Attorney General Benjamin H. Brewster decided to file suit against the Maxwell Land Grant Company.[6]

McMains's fight, meanwhile, became more personal when the land grant company took action to evict McMains from the home he was occupying within the grant boundaries. When the time came for Sheriff Allen C. Wallace to evict Oscar and Mary, the sheriff met resistance from a large crowd at the home, with some making threats against Maxwell Land Grant Company officials. Sheriff Wallace backed down.[7]

McMains restarted the *Raton Comet* (which had shut down since he sold it) and in the first new issue declared war on the Maxwell Land Grant while also going after another grant, Nolán Claim No. 39, alleging the land was in the public domain. McMains's next major move, in the fall of 1882, was to run for the territorial legislative assembly.[8] McMains was elected to the assembly, and while serving there he remained active in the lawsuit challenging the Maxwell Land Grant boundaries. Because of these obligations, he turned over the *Comet* to his partner, Charles B. Adams. Most of McMains's work as a legislator dealt with issues unrelated to land grants. After his term he did not run for reelection.[9]

In a move intended to provoke the Maxwell Land Grant Company, Oscar and Mary moved into a new home—an unoccupied ranch by Crow Creek, near Raton—that was owned by the Maxwell Land Grant Company. The company took quick legal action to have the husband and wife removed from the ranch. At a meeting in Raton, McMains announced that he would go to Washington to begin a new case challenging the size of the Maxwell Land Grant and asked for money to support his trip. When he was finally ready to go to Washington, he turned the Crow Creek ranch over to I. C. Showerman.[10]

With the case challenging the northern boundary of the Maxwell Land Grant clearly on its way to defeat, McMains filed a petition calling for a new suit against the grant company. This suit didn't claim fraud in the survey but challenged the size based on the 1869 decision that the grant must be limited to twenty-two square leagues (about one hundred and fifty square miles). He also filed a petition against Nolán Claim No. 39 on behalf of squatters living within that grant's boundaries, claiming that the Elkins and Marmon survey of Nolán Claim No. 39 had no legal status.[11]

In 1885 Grover Cleveland was inaugurated as the president of the United States of America. McMains hoped the new administration would take his side on land grant issues. He submitted yet another petition against the Maxwell Land Grant and Nolán Claim No. 39. The anti-granters received a victory when Commissioner of the General Land Office William A. J. Sparks issued the opinion that Nolán Claim No. 39 belonged in the public domain because of size limits on the amount of land allowed to be granted (the eleven leagues already being used up as part of another grant given to the same grantee, Gervacio Nolán). Secretary of the Interior Lucius Q. C. Lamar agreed with this opinion and later declared the land public domain.

Though challenged in the courts, Lamar's decision would be upheld. The victory with the opinion of Sparks concerning Nolán Claim No. 39 was followed by a defeat when a circuit court ruled in favor of the existing Maxwell Land Grant boundaries. McMains made his next appeal directly to President Cleveland. At the White House, O. P. McMains presented his case to the president. McMains left feeling positive about the meeting; however, Cleveland never got involved.[12]

The Supreme Court finally heard the Maxwell Land Grant case and on April 18, 1887, ruled in favor of the Maxwell Land Grant Company. The grant's boundaries were upheld.[13] While McMains would keep up the fight against the Maxwell Land Grant for the rest of his life, the Supreme Court decision was never overturned.

While continuing his fight against the grant boundaries, Reverend McMains was arrested in Washington. He was on the steps of the Capitol passing out circulars with charges of corruption against the commissioner of the general land grant office, James A. Williamson, Secretary of the Interior Lucius Q. C. Lamar, President Grover Cleveland, and the Supreme Court. While engaged in this, his pistol went off. The details surrounding the event are unclear, particularly due to conflicting newspaper reports.[14]

The *Washington Evening Star* reported, "While distributing these [the circulars] on the east front of the Capitol his pistol went off, but whether by accident or design is not known."[15] The *Washington Critic* report made McMains sound insane: "Quite a stir was raised at the east main door of the Capitol this morning by another crank, who had conceived the idea that the Judges of the Supreme Court should be put to death, and that it was his mission to perform the work of extermination. Before proceeding to the execution of his purpose, however, he stood on the front portico and fired several shots down the high steps without injuring any one."[16] His quick release rules out the possibility that his stated objective was a mass assassination. After his arrest he was only charged with carrying a concealed weapon.[17] Papers from around the country picked up the story. One version, repeated in several papers, said, "O. P. McMains, a crank from New Mexico, stood on the front portico of the capitol at Washington and fired five shots from a revolver at the statue of George Washington."[18]

Capitol Building, East Front Portico, circa 1885. Photographer unknown. Author's collection.

McMains soon returned home and continued his fight in New Mexico and Colorado.[19] In August 1888 Oscar McMains went to Stonewall, Colorado, because of a growing conflict between settlers in that region and the Maxwell Land Grant Company. A few hundred anti-granters gathered in Stonewall (west of Trinidad in Las Animas County) to bring attention to their grievances against the Maxwell Land Grant Company and the land they contended was public domain. In their efforts to bring attention to their cause, many of the anti-granters turned to destruction, burning the home of Maxwell Land Grant Company employee E. J. Randolph and his family. A sheriff's posse led by Deputy William Hunn arrived in town to keep the peace and prevent further property destruction.

On the morning of Saturday, August 25, a crowd of mostly masked anti-grant men approached Hunn in front of the Pooler Hotel to demand that he and the other deputies surrender their arms and leave town. O. P. McMains and Richard Russell, both unmasked, along with one or two others, met Hunn at the hotel's front door while the other deputies waited inside. Hunn, in a loud voice, told them the deputies would not go. McMains yelled to the crowd to surround the building. After they did someone in the crowd fired a gun,

Stonewall, Colorado. Date and photographer unknown. Author's collection.

which set off shooting from both sides. While Hunn quickly retreated inside, the unarmed McMains simply walked to his horse and did not participate in the fight that followed. Richard Russell was shot in the chest, the bullet entering his lung, and another man was killed on the spot.

The settlers retreated, some going behind a large barn and others behind a ridge, while Russell was taken to safety, though he would die from his wound. Shooting continued throughout the day as settlers riddled the Pooler Hotel with bullets. That night, the barn that was cover for some of the settlers caught fire. How this happened is unknown, but it was good for the deputies inside the Pooler Hotel, who used this distraction as an opportunity to sneak away through the shadow-covered grain field behind the hotel. The settlers did not discover the deputies had gone until the next day. Following all of this, Pooler Hotel was set on fire by an unknown person and destroyed.[20]

For his part in the Stonewall fight, Oscar P. McMains was indicted for manslaughter, it being charged that the crowd's actions, with McMains as their leader, is what led to Richard D. Russell's death. When McMains was brought into court, the manslaughter charge was dismissed. However, the grand jury brought ten other indictments against McMains and others, nine

Oscar P. McMains (*front, left of center*) and others outside the J. W. Shouse General Store in Stonewall, Colorado. Date and photographer unknown. Accession #CHS.X4316, History Colorado.

for assault with intent to kill and a tenth for arson (the burning of the barn). McMains was arrested again and spent one night in jail before being released on bond. It wasn't until October 12, 1889, that McMains was found not guilty on all charges. While still in the courtroom, McMains was arrested yet again, this time for conspiring to prevent the service of official papers (summonses and subpoenas).[21]

The grand jury began investigating the conspiracy charge against McMains in December 1889. He was indicted and, after a transfer of the case to Pueblo and then a postponement, the case came to trial in October of 1890. McMains was found guilty. His sentence was suspended until the next term of court, at which time O. P. McMains was sentenced to six months in the Pueblo County jail. He resumed his anti-grant activities as soon as he was released. This proved difficult as resistance to the grant had been waning for some time.[22]

Oscar and Mary McMains moved to Stonewall in 1889 and acquired an interest in mining property near there. In 1894 the Populist Party chose McMains to run for the Colorado General Assembly. He did not win a seat.[23]

Although only in his fifties, McMains's health deteriorated rapidly over the next few years until his death on April 15, 1899. He had never stopped fighting for what he believed was right, even as the battle became futile. With his wife and a few friends by his side, his last words were, "Goodbye, goodbye. I can do no more."[24]

Appendix

Franklin J. Tolby's Letters to Family

To His Niece Elizabeth Louth, December 3, 1873

Morocco, Ind., Dec. 3, 1'73

My Dear Niece: Not having heard from you for a good while, I write to inquire how all are doing, and to say that we are favored with usually good health. There's another pretty girl in the Methodist Episcopal parsonage in this place; she was born on the 22nd NOV., and is quite a fine baby if I am a competent judge. We call her *Grace*.

We were returned to this place at the last session of Conference, and are getting along well; but we have been recently appointed to the Missionary work in New Mexico, and will close up our work here within four or five weeks and, after visiting our friends, will start to Cimarron which is in the north-east part of New Mexico and near the south boundary of Colorado. Please write to Sarah Montgomery that I unfortunately neglected to answer her letter until I supposed she had left Oxford, and did not know where she might be. If she will write to me now, her letters will receive prompt attention. We shall be glad to hear from all soon.

Mary has looked for a letter from Nanie for a long time.

Yours sincerely,

F. J. Tolby

To Miss Lizzie Louth.

To His Sister Elizabeth Fisher, January 29, 1874

Cimarron, New Mexico, Jan. 29, 1'74.

My Dear Sister: We are now living in our own house, are reasonably well and very comfortably situated. Our house is built of adobes, or sun-dried bricks; in this dry climate these adobe houses are not only comfortable but substantial and beautiful. Our house contains five rooms and a hall. We are well pleased with the country and shall, perhaps, make it our home. We are kindly received by the people, and have pleasant neighbors. I preach at this place and Elizabethtown alternately. Elizabethtown is on the summit of a range of mountains among the gold mines. The valley of the Cimarron is warm and springlike in the winter, but on the mountains at Elizabethtown it is cold and the snow is deep. The valleys here are delightful to live in; the winters warm and the summers cool; one can sleep under a blanket any night in the summer. There is very little rain here except in July and August. The roads are nearly always good. Grass sustains live stock all the year round, and the people keep immense herds of cattle and flocks of sheep. Nowhere in the North-West is money made so easily as in New Mexico. The mountains are high; one in sight of our town is thirteen thousand feet high. The valleys are of two kinds; those at the foot of mountains and those up in the mountains some two thousand or three thousand feet higher than the class of valleys first named. In these upper valleys and parks the soil is fully as good as in the lower valleys; the climate is cooler and more moist, hence they produce better crops. In these lower valleys winter is so light that it would not be called winter in Indiana. In the upper valleys, cattle and sheep live nearly or quite all winter on the grass. This is a very elevated country; the valley of the Cimarron is about one mile higher than LaFayette, and, of course, the mountains are much higher; this gives us a fine atmosphere free from malarial poison. There is no ague or malarial fevers here. This is a very healthful country for such as have weak lungs unless they have consumption. The people generally appear healthy and strong, and those who have lived here three or four years seem to think that there are few countries equal to it. The Americans who live here are very intelligent—much above the average in Indiana,—but the Mexicans are ignorant and degraded. There are very few Negroes here, and the Indians—about twelve hundred in number—are to go to a reservation in the spring. The Mexicans comprise nineteen [*sic*] twentieths of the population.

We now have a fair prospect of building a railroad this year which will connect us with "the States" and bring in an American population.

Cimarron is destined to be the leading city of New Mexico. The word Cimarron is the Spanish for wild, and the city takes its name from the river. Our church's prospects are favorable. I do not recollect that I have, at any time, had stronger hope of success. The Spanish language is easily learned. I expect to be able to preach in Spanish by next new-year's day. I am glad to learn that you have an easy means of making a living, and that Shiloh is making progress at school. I hope father is well. If I succeed here as well as I hope to do, I shall be able to help him materially; and, in any case, I shall always be ready to divide with him. I had a letter from Mary, a few days ago; they are all well. I do not hear from Wiley anymore; I suppose he has "gone back on me." Mary remembers father kindly and wishes he could be with us. Rachie tells me to write to grand-pa that she and Grace are fat and rosy; and that she "loves him fifteen pounds."

Rachie is a big, healthy girl; but Gracie is a very much larger child, at the same age, and has never been sick an hour in her life; she was two months old on the 22nd of this month. Mary remains perfectly healthy; I doubt that there is a more healthy person in the world. I wish we had some good accomplished girl here for company for Mary and to help in the Sunday School; young ladies are very scarce here except Mexicans. But I fear that if we had a girl here she would soon be married to some rich old bachelor. When an attractive unmarried lady comes here she is immediately above par, Mary suggests that I ought to tell father that we have the best firewood in this country that we ever saw; it is a pleasure to build fires. Rachie has just said that if grand-pa would come here, she would go to him and would kiss him. She thinks that she would know him.

To Lizzie Fisher: Your brother, Frank.

[Notes in margins] Rachie says I must tell grand-pa to come here to live and that she loves him. When the railroad from here to a point 203 miles northeast is built, we should be within 1174 miles of Chicago and can come to LaFayette in three days' run by rail. Our firewood is of fine cedar, juniper, and pinon; the last named is the best of all. We use fireplaces instead of stoves except cook stoves, we have four fireplaces in our house. The pinon wood makes too hot a fire for a stove to stand it. We have plenty of coal but it is not needed for fuel. I formerly was much in favor of heat stones, but since I have become accustomed to sit by a good fire of dry wood on the hearth, I have "gone back" on heat stones. Mary has an excellent new cook stove. Write soon. Tell Libbie Louths [*sic*] to come; she will be welcome.

To His Niece Elizabeth Louth, April 7, 1874

Cimarron, N.M., April 7, 1'74

My Dear Niece: Your welcome letter was received some days since. We are in our usual health. We are still residing in this city. It is now a little more than three months since our arrival here, and we have, as results thus far, an organized church of five members and a Sunday School which has numbered as high as fifty. A part of our Sunday School can speak scarcely a word of English. Ours is the most satisfactory Sunday School that I have ever superintended; the little Mexicans seem to take a deep interest in the study of the Bible and the Americans study the Berean lessons without complaining that they have not time to learn them as I often heard them do in "the States." We are encouraged with the future prospect in this beautiful country. We have had very few cold days this winter, and it is considered by the old settlers the coldest for seven years past. The Rocky Mountains as they enter this territory spread out into the Sierra Madre; yet not so as to prevent our constructing good roads and having convenient access to all important points. The valleys in many cases are exceedingly fertile; I know of a valley which has been cultivated about two hundred years, and which still produces good crops; and yet the indolent Mexicans who own it have never hauled a load of fertilizers on it. The agricultural lands in this territory consist of valley lands and park lands; of course, you know what valley lands are; but the park lands you may not so well comprehend. Let me describe; you go into a valley; you discover a creek flowing down from among the mountains; you follow up towards the source of that stream; you find a tract of level land in the midst of the mountains and surrounded by the mountains; this is a park. A large portion of the surface of this territory is mountainous; and many of the mountains are full of silver, iron, copper, and coal, gold exists in large quantities in the Moreno Mountains which are near us. I preach once in two weeks in the Moreno mining camp. The climate is very different in different parts; in the valleys cattle live on the wild grass through the winter, in the parks excellent grass grows but is more likely to be covered by snow in the winter. The winters are warm, the summers, cool. The elevation of the country is very great, otherwise it would be much warmer. In some parts of the territory, fruits can be produced as nowhere else on this side of the Pacific coast. In the Mesilla valley, a root graft planted ten years ago is now an apple tree twelve inches in diameter and yields forty bushels of apples. In the valley of the Rio Grande, we produce wine as good, perhaps, as any produced in France. Grapes flourish in many parts of the Rio Grande valley; of this I am assured by Hon. J. G. Palen, Chief Justice of this territory. I presume this is a better country for grapes than any of the States east of it. In some parts of the territory, fruits can not be raised at all. The best part of the territory for fruit is the Southern part; there winter is warmer and the summer not cool enough to injure fruit. Any man can find in one part or another of this territory what he wants in the way of a country. We never have ague or malarial fevers in New Mexico. If one who has weak lungs comes to this territory before tubercular consumption has commenced, it is believed that he will, almost invariably, get well. In the Mesilla valley, land in abundance can yet be had by homesteading, and Mexican ranches can be bought for little more than entrance price. I will send your pa some of our N. Mexico newspapers. Our love to all.

Very respectfully, Your Uncle Frank.

[Notes in margins] It would amuse you to hear Rachie speak Spanish words. Rachie has just kissed me, saying that she kissed me instead of kissing aunt Sat. because she could not kiss her. She now tells me to write, "come here aunt Sat. and then 'I will kiss you.'"

To Elizabeth Louth, July 29, 1874

Cimarron, N.M., July 29, '74

My Dear Niece: Not having heard from you for a good while, I have
thought that I would write again to say that we are still in our usual health,
and alive notwithstanding Indian hostilities. The hostile bands have not been
nearer than twelve miles of our town. They have killed about thirty of our
people, and have driven off many horses and mules; but we think that we
have them now, under control. I furnished dispatches to the Inter-Ocean in
which you may learn particulars. Our church-work is not much changed since
last writing. The Indians, resident in our (Colfax) County, remain friendly
and assisted us in the war. We feel comparatively safe now, and hope that
we shall have no further trouble with the Indians who recently made war
on our country. The Indian war has raged along hundreds of miles of the
South-western border on which Cimarron stands. The Indians are afraid to
attack houses; therefore no one has been killed in a house. They know that the
men of this border are not to be trifled with, therefore a house could hardly
be taken without an Indian being killed, and they do not take such chances;
but if they can catch a man out herding his cattle or sheep or traveling on the
road, they kill him. For several days, we lived in apprehension of an attack
on any evening or morning; at such times, they make their attacks, usually.
At the hour of retiring, I made my arrangements for battle. One evening when
we had put the children in bed and Mary had lain down by them, and when
I was about ready to extinguish the light in our room, it was discovered that
I had forgotten to bring into the room as usual, a certain weapon of defense;
Rachie thought that would not do, and said, "Papa, if you do not bring in
your 'volver, the first thing you know you will see that some big Indian will
get your girls." Rachie is quite a bright little girl and grows more beautiful
every year. She directs me to write to you that she loves Sabbath School,
knows a portion of the alphabet, prays everyday, and has a new chromo, and
loves you. Little Gracie is large of [*sic*] her age, fat as a china pig, and is
very much like Rachie. We have delightful summer weather in New Mexico.
The summers are as much cooler that [*sic*] the summers in Indiana, as the
winters are warmer. We have very few house-flies; I saw one on my table this

morning, at breakfast. The country is very beautiful; I think it will make me as strong as an ox. Whoever has weak lungs in which tubercules have not yet formed, should come to New Mexico. Please write soon.

To Lizzie Louth.   Yours very truly, F.J. Tolby

P.S. Have you heard from Mary Henderson of late? Mary—that is, my Mary, will write Nannie, soon; she would have written long ago, but for the fact that the babies require about all her time. Give Nannie our regards and tell her that we should be glad to receive letters from her often. Say to that "fine boy" that I am coming to see him, sometime. Yours etc, F. J. T.

Copies of letters from New Mexico Annual Conference of the United Methodist Church Archives.

Letter to the *New York Sun*, Written June 2, 1875

The following letter, written on June 2 and published on July 5, 1875, was believed by many to have been written by Franklin Tolby. On February 7, 1876, a statement was published in the *Sun* denying that Tolby had written the letter.

TERRITORY OF ELKINS

THE PETTY DESPOTISM THAT IS CALLED NEW MEXICO

A Ring-Ridden People—The Population of a Whole Territory at the Mercy of a Firm of Sharp Lawyers—An Opportunity for Attorney-General Edwards Pierrepont.

SANTA FE, New Mexico, June 2.—The renomination by the Republican Convention, yesterday, of that unctuous individual, S. B. Elkins, as candidate for delegate to Congress, makes a fitting text for some remarks relative to the politics and people of New Mexico, the more especially as this Territory is claimed as the stronghold of Republicanism and Grantism in the far West. The Mexican population are easily controlled, and it is rare for even an educated and wealthy Mexican to take the lead in any movement. This is not surprising. For twenty-five years prior to the acquisition of the country by the United States, New Mexico had been in a state of continual turmoil. Civil wars had rendered it a constantly active political volcano. Nine-tenths of the people were in a form of slavery called peonage, and all the property was in the hands of a few wealthy individuals. Few, even of the wealthy classes, were educated, and the masses grovelled [*sic*] in ignorance and poverty.

In this condition the United States found the country in 1846, and at once established a strong, stable Government, sustained for a time by military power, and substituted law and order for the chaos which had reigned. The effect of this new order of things was to impress the people with an almost superstitious respect and awe for the forms of law, and the officials who administered it. A local magistrate had always been a great man among the people, but a United States Judge, having the power of the Government at his back to enforce his decrees, was looked upon as little less than a king. And this feeling is prevalent here to this day. Nothing is so eagerly sought for by a Mexican as a place on a jury. Nothing is so terrible to him as the threat of an indictment. To attain the one he will make almost any promise, while to escape the other he will barter his soul.

IMPROVING THE OPPORTUNITIES

We have here, therefore, all the conditions requisite for a carpet-bag Government of the most orthodox description, and we have one which, by reason of its remoteness from the capital, has become almost wholly irresponsible and absolute. The population of the Territory consists of about 100,000 Mexicans, and perhaps 5,000 Americans, the number of voters being 17,000, many of whom are roving miners, who take little interest in politics. Furthermore, the greater portion of the valuable lands were owned by wealthy Mexicans, deriving their titles through grants of immense tracts by the Mexican Government. Many, if not most, of these titles were imperfect, and much trouble and expense were often required to establish them. In these matters the power and influence of United States officials was highly estimated, and correspondingly respected and feared by the wealthy, through whom the poorer classes, still in practical serfdom, though no longer peons, were absolutely controlled. These conditions afforded a rare opportunity for demagogues and carpet-baggers, and that there were not wanting men to take advantage of it.

AN ENTERPRISING FIRM

I will introduce to the reader the law firm of Elkins & Catron and their co-ringmasters. The advent of Elkins to New Mexico dates about the year 1863 or 1864, and is said to have been hastened by reason of his having served his country in both the Confederate and Federal home guards about Lexington and Westport, Missouri. It would seem that his success, financial and otherwise, was not great, until, after the close of the war, he was joined by his friend and former schoolmate, then plain Tom Catron, ex-lieutenant of artillery in the Confederate army. Then the affairs of the twain began to prosper, and each became a member of the Legislature and Attorney-General in turn. But it was not until the arrival of the Hon. Jos. G. Palen, member of the National Republican Committee and ex-Postmaster at Albany, N. Y., as Chief Justice of the Federal and District Courts of the Territory, in 1868, that their success culminated. Since that time, and especially since the accession of the Hon. Hezek S. Johnson, formerly known as Blue Dick, as Judge of the Second Judicial District, whereby Palen and Johnson constituted a majority of the bench of the Supreme Court, that the affairs of Elkins & Catron, attorneys at law, have been in a flourishing condition.

A BACK PAY GRAB

The success of Elkins & Catron seems to have been materially promoted about this time by their ability to secure the passage of a back pay grab bill by the Legislature, whereby the legislators voted themselves out of the territorial treasury $5 per diem salary in addition to that paid by the Government. As the treasury was not provided with funds for such a contingency, territorial scrip was issued instead. The legislators, however, did not reap much benefit, since the issue of such a quantity of paper, to redeem which there were no funds, soon brought the value of territorial scrip down to 15 or 20 cents on the dollar. These patriotic lawyers then came forward with their friends and relieved the holders of the scrip by investing their hard-earned pennies at the figures named. The holders thought themselves well rid of the stuff, until the next session, when the patriots had influence enough to pass a law funding the scrip into territorial bonds, bearing 100 percent, interest, and also a tax law to provide means for their payment. Having cleared about $40,000 by this transaction, the fortunes of the firm were at high tide. In fact, it is a subject of general remark that to win a suit in the territorial courts requires the employment of the services of both members of the firm, since if only one is retained the adverse party employs the other, and when the suit is ended neither client has anything left after paying courts costs.

A NICE ARRANGEMENT

One or the other of these eminent counsellors [*sic*] is always United States prosecuting attorney. This lucrative office was filled for a long time by the senior member of the firm; but in 1872 his ambition soared to a loftier height, and he determined to represent his people at the Capitol of the nation, whereupon the junior was invested with the dignities of the office, which was used as a doubled-barreled weapon. The junior went to prosecuting, and the senior to defending. When Elkins was nominated for Congress in 1873, his retainers were summoned to Santa Fe, as jurors and witnesses in the United States Court, and the convention waxed enthusiastic under the stimulus of jury fees and mileage.

Recalcitrant Republicans and influential Democrats were indicted for crimes of various descriptions. Their cases were continued until after election. They voted for Elkins, and achieved their liberty. In many parts of the Territory there are grants of land inhabited by communities of Pueblos, of civilized Indians who are descendants of the original Mexicans. They had been recognized as citizens, capable of holding property, by Mexico, and had been repeatedly decided to be such by the courts of New Mexico. Their grants had been confirmed and set apart to them by the United States. In many cases, portions of these lands had been settled by Mexicans, with the consent of the owners, either under lease or purchase. Now there is a United States statute which prohibits, under penalty of $1,000, any person settling upon an Indian reservation. Furthermore, the politics of many of these settlers upon Pueblo lands was doubtful. They were not altogether sound on the Elkins question. United States Attorney Catron thereupon

COMMENCED PROSECUTIONS

against some 600 of these unfortunate individuals. Notwithstanding previous decisions, that these were not Indian reservations, it was said that there was no escape for the culprits except through the employment of Elkins to defend them, and the suggestion was acted on. These cases, too, were continued until after [the] election. The defendants voted for Elkins. Nobody was convicted, but there are people who say that the United States Attorney received $20 from the Government for each of these prosecutions, making the refreshing sum of $12,000, besides the pleasure of helping his friend to 600 votes.

When Col. John Hittson made his celebrated raid into New Mexico in 1872 with an armed troop of Texans, taking by force all cattle found in the country bearing certain brands, Elkins & Catron were the legal advisers of the expedition, and as the election for delegate approached, they procured from the Governor of Texas requisitions for the arrest, on charge of cattle stealing, of certain citizens of New Mexico, who, though they had never in their lives been in the State of Texas, and could not be guilty of the offence charged, were guilty of a far greater crime. They were not supporting Elkins. To be taken to Texas on such a charge was understood to be, in view of the excited feeling there on the subject of cattle thieving, almost certain death. The parties named in the requisitions were not arrested, but it was observable that they all became enthusiastic Elkins men. One of these parties, for instance, who did not work well in the harness before the receipt of the requisition, marched 135 Mexicans in solid column to the polls, and voted them for Elkins.

ANOTHER MEANS FOR SECURING VOTES

was found in the fact that the holders of claims against the Government for Indian depredations, war supplies, &c., to the amount of several millions, and also claimants of the large land grants, nearly all of which were and are in litigation, had discovered the unbounded influence of the Ring in the courts, and also its power to harm their interests before the departments at Washington, especially in that controlled by Delano and his son John. Consequently, as a measure of self-protection, they had been compelled to place their interests in the hands of the Ring lawyers. To withdraw them was considered to be fatal, and to fail in support of the Radical candidate was fully as bad. Hence all these people, to make the best of a bad job, voted for Elkins. Civil suits were compromised against clients' wishes and interests, and, in short, the whole machinery of the courts and the Federal offices was directed and used to accomplish the election of Elkins. So Elkins went to Congress, and Catron remained to run the affairs of the firm here, and its business, especially in claims against the Government, flourished with renewed vigor, with one member at each end of the line.

But so questionable were the means and influences employed to accomplish this end that it became evident soon after the election that active steps would have to be taken to prevent a reaction, and accordingly the machinery of the Legislature was put in operation to fortify the ground already gained.

There is a peculiarity in the proceedings of New Mexico Legislatures which is worth noting. When a bill is before one of its august branches, and on its passage, the usual custom of debating its merits is rarely resorted to, but the practice is for the supporters of the bill to move for a recess of ten minutes or half an hour, which is almost always carried. What takes place during this intermission is not reported in the records, but as the offices of the principal members of the Ring are conveniently located, and as many of the members seem to prefer them as loafing places to the legislative halls, it is proba-ble that convincing arguments are employed to secure the needed number of votes. However this may be, it is certain that immediately following some of these recesses measures were passed in the Ring interest which will darken the pages of New Mexican history for long years.

THE LITTLE GAME OF CHUZAS

One of these was the infamous chuzas law. What chuzas is, I am unable to state, further than that it is a kind of gambling game which is a favorite pastime of the Mexican, who has a natural love for games of hazard. This game was legalized by the act—gambling being generally forbidden by law—and immediately it became the rage throughout the Territory. It is well to note that the Ring lawyers, in and out of the Legislature, supported the bill. About a month later, when thousands were nightly enjoying the fascination of the game, the court decided, that though legalized, it was still illegal, and the Attorney-General proceeded to file hundreds of informations against those who had been indulging in the sport. This was a bombshell in the chuzas camp, but a larger one fell when it was learned that in the mean time spies had made lists of the names of most of the players. Among the victims was the Governor, who, rumor said, had gambled off a twenty-five cent piece of fractional currency, given him by his wife to buy beefsteak for breakfast. He fell among the rest before the wiles and tricks of this Ring, who pocketed thousands in the way of court and prosecuting attorneys' fees, and added greatly to their powers of terrifying the natives.

THE NEXT OUTRAGE

consisted in the passage of a law by which a delinquent taxpayer became not only liable to a civil suit for unpaid taxes, with all its attendant costs and fees; to have his property sold summarily by the sheriff, but also to be arrested, convicted and punished as a criminal. He was liable to either or all these proceedings as the officials might deem proper. Thus, for failure to pay his taxes by a certain day, he could be compelled to pay the tax with interest, court and attorney's fees for collection, and be fined and imprisoned besides. No excuse can save him if the fixed date is once passed. Even non-residents, owning property here, are indicted, and may be arrested whenever they set foot on the soil of New Mexico. Now, as taxation is a new thing to the Mexicans—the territorial Government having been supported by licenses and special taxes prior to the accession of the Ring to power—and they being generally wholly unaware of the effect of the law, or perhaps of its existence, thousands become delinquent, and at present the courts are busy with indictments and informations for this offence, which will be held over the heads of the unfortunates till after election, when they will be dismissed with costs and attorneys' fees if the poor devils vote for Elkins.

THE WORST OF ALL

But the most oppressive act of all saddled upon these unhappy people by the conspirators was a law regarding the practice in civil suits, whereby a party was enabled to bring a suit in any county of the judicial district in which either he or the defendant resides and five days' notice, either personal or served by leaving a copy at the defendant's house, whether he or his family are at home or not, constitutes legal service. Now, when it is understood that the average size of a judicial district is 300 miles by 150, and that nineteen-twentieths of the Territory has no other means of conveyance than by saddle or wagon, over rough mountain roads; and further, that a large portion of the people are most of the time away from home with their herds, it will be readily seen that in many cases it is simply impossible for a party sued to appear and defend his case, or employ an attorney, for want of time, before judgment is rendered by default. And, as it rests entirely with the Ring's court as to whether a case may be continued for want of time to get evidence, some most glaring cases of oppression and injustice occur, while no redress is obtainable. The effect of the law is that if any one opposes the Ring, he is liable at any moment to have his property levied on by the Sheriff and sold under a judgment, the existence of which he never knew.

THE NEWSPAPER PRESS

seems to be in a complete state of subjection, and does nothing to remedy the evils herein pointed out. I venture to state that not a single newspaper in the Territory dares to express its views, if in conflict with the Ring interests. Members of the editorial fraternity are fined and jailed until they are convinced that silence is the most discreet policy, and that any show of boldness, honesty, or independence in their treatment of the conduct and measures of the radical Ring bring only incarceration and distress.

In conversation with many of the leading citizens of the Territory I find that almost universally this Ring is despised and detested, and that its overthrow is anxiously hoped for. But while all desire that end, but few can be found who dare to take the lead in encountering the many-headed monster. There is no doubt but that the voters would destroy it at the polls, so far as depends on local elections, were it not that by the registration law, as enforced here, every man's vote becomes public, or at least known to the Ring, and if it is hostile, the voter becomes from that moment a marked man, liable to have an indictment hurled at him at the next court. Besides this, the elections are largely controlled by the Ring through manipulation of the ballot boxes; and if a man votes adversely to it, there is no certainty that his vote will not be replaced by a fraudulent one.

There are some, I believe, among the territorial officials who honestly desire a reform, and if certain of success would labor for that end. But the courts constitute the great engine which propels the Ring's affairs, and these would-be-honest people fear to encounter this power, as failure would insure the loss of their places. Others again are entirely incapable of doing good or harm, being political hacks who are sent out here from the East to get them out of the way.

A GLEAM OF HOPE

is now visible, however, in the political horizon. The removal of Landaulet Williams and the appointment of Mr. Pierrepont as Attorney General, lead many to hope for a speedy displacement of the men who disgrace the Department of Justice in this Territory. Another important fact is the ignominious defeat in Congress of Elkins's pet scheme, whereby New Mexico was to be admitted as a State, and he be chosen Senator. For a time it was considered certain that he would succeed in this project, but having failed in that, and failed to procure any legislation of real benefit to the Territory when so much was needed, the people begin to think that he is not such a power in Washington as he has claimed to be.

The county organizations, where not in the absolute grasp of the Ring, already begin to show signs of discontent. This discontent and insubordination have been manifested to such a degree in some of the counties that, to insure the nomination of Elkins at yesterday's convention, it was necessary to hold the primary conventions in an almost secret manner, and to have present only a few, who, being under indictment or otherwise bound to support the Ring, could be relied upon. Indeed, unless sufficient terrorism can be excited by the courts, or the ballot boxes are tampered with to an unusual extent, there is a strong probability that the party of Grant and the Ring will meet a crushing defeat at the fall election.

Endnotes

Notes for Chapter 1

1. Thomas E. Chávez, *An Illustrated History of New Mexico* (Albuquerque: University of New Mexico Press, 1992), 10–11; Leon Metz, *Border: The U.S.–Mexico Line* (Fort Worth: TCU Press, 2008), 83; White, Koch, Kelley, and McCarthy, Attorneys at Law, *Land Title Study* (Santa Fe: New Mexico State Planning Office, 1971), 25 and 27; L. Bradford Prince, *The Student's History of New Mexico* (Denver: Publishers Press, 1921), 123.

2. *Treaty of Guadalupe Hidalgo: Definition and List of Community Land Grants in New Mexico* (Washington, DC: United States General Accounting Office, 2001), 3, 6, 7, and 22–29; *Treaty of Guadalupe Hidalgo: Findings and Possible Options Regarding Longstanding Community Land Grant Claims in New Mexico* (Washington, DC: United States General Accounting Office, 2004), 14.

3. *Definition and List of Community Land Grants in New Mexico*, 1 and 3–5.

4. María Montoya, *Translating Property: The Maxwell Land Grant and the Conflict over Land in the American West, 1840–1900* (Berkeley: University of California Press, 2002), 49; Corey Recko, "Samuel B. Axtell and the Colfax County War: Axtell's 'Dear Ben' Letter," *Wild West History Association Journal* 2, no. 2 (April 2009): 43.

5. William H. Wroth, "Maxwell Land Grant," *New Mexico History: State Records Center & Archives*, accessed April 1, 2024, http://newmexicohistory.org/places/maxwell-land-grant; Montoya, *Translating Property*, 30; *The Supreme Court Reporter*, vol. 7, *Cases Argued and Determined in the United States Supreme Court, October Term, 1886* (St. Paul: West Publishing Company, 1887), 1016.

6. William A. Keleher, *Maxwell Land Grant: A New Mexico Item* (Albuquerque: University of New Mexico Press, 1942), 26–27; Harriet Freiberger, "Lucien Maxwell: From Cimarron to Fort Sumner," *History Net*, March 1, 2017, http://www.historynet.com/lucien-maxwell-cimarron-fort-sumner.htm; Kathleen P. Chamberlain, "Billy the Kid, Susan McSween, Thomas Catron, and the Modernization of New Mexico, 1865-1912," chap. 7 in *New Mexican Lives: Profiles and Historical Stories*, ed. Richard W. Etulain (Albuquerque: University

of New Mexico Press, 2002), 200; Norman Cleaveland and George Fitzpatrick, *The Morleys: Young Upstarts on the Southwest Frontier* (Albuquerque: Calvin Horn, 1971), 61–62; Montoya, *Translating Property,* 62; F. Stanley, "O. P. McMains, Champion of a Lost Cause," *New Mexico Historical Review* 24 (January 1949): 2.

7. Chamberlain, "Billy the Kid," 200; Wroth, "Maxwell Land Grant"; Freiberger, "Lucien Maxwell."

8. Chamberlain, "Billy the Kid," 200; "Elkins, Stephen Benton (1841–1911)," *Biographical Directory of the United States Congress,* accessed 2014, http://bioguide.congress.gov/scripts/biodisplay.pl?index=E000110; Victor Westphall, *Thomas Benton Catron and His Era* (Tucson: University of Arizona Press, 1973), 100.

9. Cleaveland and Fitzpatrick, *Morleys,* 49–50; Westphall, *Thomas Benton Catron,* 100–101.

10. Cleaveland and Fitzpatrick, *Morleys,* 62; Jim Berry Pearson, *The Maxwell Land Grant* (Norman: University of Oklahoma Press, 1961), 49–50; Westphall, *Thomas Benton Catron,* 100–101; David L. Caffey, *Frank Springer and New Mexico: From the Colfax County War to the Emergence of Modern Santa Fe* (College Station: Texas A&M University Press, 2006), 16; *Transcript of Title of the Maxwell Land Grant Situated in New Mexico and Colorado* (Chicago: Rand McNally, 1881), 62–63; *The Supreme Court Reporter,* vol. 14, *Cases Argued and Determined in the United States Supreme Court, October Term, 1893* (St. Paul: West Publishing Company, 1894), 459; R. F. Pettit Jr., "Maxwell Land Grant," in *Taos-Raton-Spanish Peaks Country (New Mexico and Colorado): New Mexico Geological Society 17th Annual Fall Field Conference Guidebook,* edited by S. A. Northrop and C. B. Read, 66–68 (Socorro, NM: New Mexico Geological Society, 1966) https://nmgs.nmt.edu/publications/guidebooks/downloads/17/17_p0066_p0068.pdf. Maxwell's Cimarron mansion was excluded from the original purchase but was soon after bought by the Maxwell Land Grant and Railway Company.

11. Contract between Alexander P. Sullivan and the Maxwell Land Grant and Railway Company to establish a newspaper at Cimarron, September 22, 1870, box 45, folder 4, Maxwell Land Grant Company Records, Center for Southwest Research, University of New Mexico, Albuquerque, NM (hereafter cited as Maxwell Land Grant Records); Pearson, Maxwell Land Grant, 63; Howard R. Lamar, "The Santa Fe Ring," chap. 13 in *New Mexico, Past and Present: A Historical*

Reader, ed. Richard N. Ellis (Albuquerque: University of New Mexico Press, 1971), 153; Robert W. Larson, *New Mexico Populism: A Study of Radical Protest in a Western Territory* (Boulder: Colorado Associated University Press, 1974), 23; Lawrence R. Murphy, *Philmont: A History of New Mexico's Cimarron County* (Albuquerque: University of New Mexico Press, 1972), 121; Pearson, *Maxwell Land Grant*, 50; Freiberger, "Lucien Maxwell."

12. John Collinson, *The Maxwell Land Grant, Situated in Colorado and New Mexico, United States of America* (London: Taylor and Co., 1870), 31–32; "Benjamin, Judah Philip (1811–1884)," *Biographical Directory of the United States Congress*, accessed 2008, http://bioguide.congress.gov/scripts/biodisplay.pl?index=b000365.

13. Chamberlain, "Billy the Kid," 200; David J. Wishart, ed., *Encyclopedia of the Great Plains* (Lincoln: University of Nebraska Press, 2004), 361; *Supreme Court Reporter*, 7:1016; *Raton Weekly Independent*, April 21, 1888.

14. Pearson, *Maxwell Land Grant*, 61; Westphall, *Thomas Benton Catron*, 101.

15. *Santa Fe Daily New Mexican*, October 28 and 31, 1870, and April 17, 1871; Pearson, *Maxwell Land Grant*, 63 and 65; Murphy, *Philmont*, 117–18.

16. F. Stanley, *The Elizabethtown, New Mexico Story* (Dumas, TX: F. Stanley, 1961), 3–4 and 9; Philip Varney, *New Mexico's Best Ghost Towns: A Practical Guide* (Albuquerque: University of New Mexico Press, 1987), 39–40; Kathy Weiser-Alexander, "Elizabethtown: Gone but Not Forgotten," *Legends of America*, updated July 2023, http://www.legendsofamerica.com/nm-etown.html.

17. Contract between the Maxwell Land Grant and Railway Company and William R. Morley, November 11, 1872, box 20, folder 3, Maxwell Land Grant Records; Cleaveland and Fitzpatrick, *Morleys*, 40–41, 49–50, 51, 53, 57, and 68; 1855 Massachusetts State Census for Blandford, Hampden County, MA: Dorcas S. S. Morley and William R. Morley; Ancestry.com page for William Raymond Morley by William Wohlers; *Roster and Record of Iowa Soldiers in the War of the Rebellion*, vol. 2 (Des Moines: Emory H. English, State Printer, 1908), 3 and 94; Walter R. Borneman, *Iron Horses: America's Race to Bring the Railroads West* (New York: Back Bay Books / Little, Brown, 2014), 131; Agnes Morley Cleaveland, *No Life for a Lady* (Lincoln: University of Nebraska Press, 1977), 5 and 6.

18. Pearson, *Maxwell Land Grant*, 59; Westphall, *Thomas Benton Catron*, 108 and 109; Cleaveland and Fitzpatrick, *Morleys*, 75.

19. Geoffrey Perret, *Ulysses S. Grant: Soldier and President* (New York: Random House, 1997), 420; Josiah Bunting III, *Ulysses S. Grant* (New York: Times Books, Henry Holt and Company, 2004), 140; "Panic of 1873," U-S-History.com, accessed 2010, http://www.u-s-history.com/pages/h213.html.

20. Cleaveland and Fitzpatrick, *Morleys*, 75–77; Pearson, *Maxwell Land Grant*, 57–58; *Railroad Gazette: A Journal of Transportation, Engineering and Railroad News, Seventeenth Year* (New York: Railroad Gazette, 1873), 435.

21. Cleaveland and Fitzpatrick, *Morleys*, 71–72.

22. Cleaveland and Fitzpatrick, *Morleys*, 71–72; Pearson, *Maxwell Land Grant*, 59.

23. Pearson, *Maxwell Land Grant*, 65; Larson, *New Mexico Populism*, 24; *Santa Fe Daily New Mexican*, April 2, 1873.

24. Cleaveland and Fitzpatrick, *Morleys*, 72–73; Westphall, *Thomas Benton Catron*, 109; Caffey, *Frank Springer and New Mexico*, 4, 5, 7, 8–9, 10–11, 13, 18, 19, and 20.

25. Pearson, *Maxwell Land Grant*, 65–66.

26. Cleaveland, *No Life for a Lady*, 7–8; Cleaveland and Fitzpatrick, *Morleys*, 83; deposition of Frank Springer, August 9, 1878, Frank W. Angel Report on the Charges against Samuel B. Axtell (hereafter cited as Angel Report against Axtell), Governor of New Mexico, Interior Department Appointment Papers (hereafter cited as Int. Dept. Appt. Papers), Territory of New Mexico, 1850–1907, RG 48, National Archives and Records Administration, College Park, MD (hereafter cited as NARA).

27. Pearson, *Maxwell Land Grant*, 59–60; F. Stanley, *The Grant That Maxwell Bought* (Denver: World Press, 1952), 92; Keleher, *Maxwell Land Grant*, 59–65.

Notes for Chapter 2

1. Robert W. Larson, *New Mexico's Quest for Statehood, 1846–1912* (Albuquerque: University of New Mexico Press, 1968), 121–23; *History of New Mexico: Its Resources and People, Illustrated*, vol. 1 (Los Angeles: Pacific States, 1907), 156–57; L. Bradford Prince, *A Concise History of New Mexico* (Cedar Rapids: Torch Press, 1914), 231–32;

Journal of the Senate of the United States of America, vol. 70 (Washington, DC: Government Printing Office, 1875), 339; *Journal of the House of Representatives of the United States*, vol. 74 (Washington, DC: Government Printing Office, 1874), 1010–11, and vol. 75 (Washington, DC: Government Printing Office, 1875), 644–46. The number of no votes for the New Mexico statehood bill has often been reported as eighty-seven due to a counting error in the *Journal of the House of Representatives of the United States*.

2. Prince, *Concise History of New Mexico*, 232; *History of New Mexico*, 1:156–57.
3. *Journal of the House of Representatives*, 75:632.
4. Larson, *New Mexico's Quest for Statehood*, 124–25; *New York Times*, March 5, 1875.
5. Cleaveland and Fitzpatrick, *Morleys*, 84–87.
6. Cleaveland and Fitzpatrick, *Morleys*, 87.
7. Ralph E. Twitchell, *Leading Facts of New Mexican History*, vol. 2 (Cedar Rapids: Torch Press, 1912), 397–98; *Minutes of the New Mexico Bar Association, Fifth Annual Session, Together with Constitution and By-Laws as Amended and in Force January 31, 1890* (Santa Fe: New Mexican Printing Company, 1890), 47–48.
8. Twitchell, *Leading Facts*, 2:401–2; "Elkins, Stephen Benton"; David L. Caffey, *Chasing the Santa Fe Ring: Power and Privilege in Territorial New Mexico* (Albuquerque: University of New Mexico Press, 2014), 19, 21, and 88; Westphall, *Thomas Benton Catron*, 6; Oscar Doane Lambert, *Stephen Benton Elkins* (Pittsburgh: University of Pittsburgh Press, 1955), 11; *Journal of the Senate of the State of Missouri at the Regular Session of the Twenty-Third General Assembly* (Jefferson City: W. A. Curry, Public Printer, 1865), 525.
9. Westphall, *Thomas Benton Catron*, 109–10.
10. Caffey, *Chasing the Santa Fe Ring*, 88–89.
11. Twitchell, *Leading Facts of New Mexican History*, 2:519–20; Frederick Nolan, *The Lincoln County War: A Documentary History* (Norman: University of Oklahoma Press, 1992), 450–51; Westphall, *Thomas Benton Catron*, 6; "Catron, Thomas Benton, (1840–1921)," *Biographical Directory of the United States Congress*, accessed 2008, http://bioguide.congress.gov/scripts/biodisplay.pl?index=c000253.
12. Cleaveland and Fitzpatrick, *Morleys*, 84; Caffey, *Frank Springer and New Mexico*, 25.

13. Cleaveland and Fitzpatrick, *Morleys*, 89 and 91; Thomas Henry Tibbles, *Buckskin and Blanket Days* (Garden City, NY: Doubleday & Company, 1957), 17–18; 1850 Federal Census for Hancock, IL: Mary E. Tibbles; 1870 Federal Census for Pottawattamie, IA: M. E. McPherson; 1880 Federal Census for Washington, DC: Mary McPherson; Deaths Registered in the city of Boston in 1897, Mary McPherson, accessed 2018, https://www.ancestry.com/discoveryui-content/view/2217979:2101?tid=&pid=&queryId=241ec575-73d3-4f4f-bd7b-12d2abb92c95&_phsrc=JdZ13&_phstart=successSource.

14. Cleaveland and Fitzpatrick, *Morleys*, 87; deposition of Springer, August 9, 1878, Angel Report against Axtell, Int. Dept. Appt. Papers; Westphall, *Thomas Benton Catron*, 116.

15. Deposition of Springer, August 9, 1878, Angel Report against Axtell, Int. Dept. Appt. Papers; Lamar, "Santa Fe Ring" in Ellis, *New Mexico, Past and Present*, 156; *History of New Mexico*, 1:322; Cleaveland and Fitzpatrick, *Morleys*, 92.

16. Deposition of Asa F. Middaugh, March 31, 1876, Angel Report against Axtell, Int. Dept. Appt. Papers; Cleaveland, *No Life for a Lady*, 9.

17. Cleaveland and Fitzpatrick, *Morleys*, 95–96; Morris F. Taylor, *O. P. McMains and the Maxwell Land Grant Conflict* (Tucson: University of Arizona Press, 1979), 37; *Santa Fe Daily New Mexican*, June 1 and 7, 1875; Leo E. Oliva, *Fort Union and the Frontier Army in the Southwest: A Historical Resource* (Santa Fe, NM: Division of History, National Park Service, 1993), 395.

18. Cleaveland and Fitzpatrick, *Morleys*, 96–97; Taylor, *O. P. McMains*, 37; deposition of Springer, August 9, 1878, Angel Report against Axtell, Int. Dept. Appt. Papers; testimony of William Low, Isaiah Rinehart, Irvin W. Lacy, and S. Erastus Welding, as reported in an undated copy of the *Cimarron News and Press*, Int. Dept. Appt. Papers; Caffey, *Frank Springer and New Mexico*, 28; *Register of Officers and Agents, Civil, Military, and Naval, in the Service of the United States on the Thirtieth of September, 1875* (Washington, DC: Government Printing Office, 1876), 367; 1880 United Stated Federal Census for Part of Rayado Precinct No. 4, Colfax County, NM: Cipriano Lara.

19. Keleher, William A., *Violence in Lincoln County, 1869–1881, a New Mexico Item* (Albuquerque: University of New Mexico Press, 1957), 21 and 25; John A. Garraty and Mark C. Carnes, eds., *American National Biography*, 24 vols. (New York: Oxford University Press, 1999), 1:785.

20. Garraty and Carnes, *American National Biography*, 1:784–85; "Axtell, Samuel Beach (1819–1891)," *Biographical Directory of the United States Congress*, accessed 2011, http://bioguide.congress.gov/scripts/biodisplay.pl?index=A000349; Axtell, Ephraim S., *The Axtell Record: Being a Family Record of the Descendants of Maj. Henry Axtell of Mendham, Morris Co., New Jersey, Who Lived from 1738 to 1818* (Morristown, NJ: Jerseyman, 1886), 31; 1860 Federal Census for Township No. 1, County of Amador, CA: S. B. Axtell.

21. B. H. Roberts, *A Comprehensive History of the Church of Jesus Christ of Latter-day Saints*, vol. 5, *Century 1* (Provo: Brigham Young University Press, 1965), 595–600; Garraty and Carnes, *American National Biography*, 1:785; Wayne Stout, *History of Utah*, vol. 1, *1870–1896* (Salt Lake City: Wayne Stout, 1907), 58; Keleher, *Violence in Lincoln County*, 23 and 25–26; the *Salt Lake Daily Tribune*, February 16, 1875.

22. Taylor, *O. P. McMains*, 37.

23. "The Territory of Elkins," *New York Sun*, July 5, 1875.

24. "The Territory of Elkins," *New York Sun*, July 5, 1875.

25. Simeon H. Newman III, "The Santa Fe Ring: A Letter to the *New York Sun*," *Arizona and the West* 12, no. 3 (Autumn 1970): 269–88; Kristi Smith, "S. H. Newman: Pioneer Newspaperman Fought Vice," *Borderlands* 22 (2003–2004), http://epcc.libguides.com/content.php?pid=309255&sid=2604083.

26. "A Most Audacious Ring," *New York Sun*, August 16, 1875.

Notes for Chapter 3

1. Rose A. Taulbee, *Taulbee: The History of the Taulbee Family in America* (Denver: Andrew Burt, 2006), 18, 21–22; *Minutes of the Annual Conferences of the Methodist Episcopal Church for the Year 1872* (New York: Nelson & Phillips, 1872), 75; *Minutes of the Annual Conferences of the Methodist Episcopal Church for the Year 1876* (New York: Nelson & Phillips, 1876), 367; Civil War Pension Record for James F. Talby [*sic*], alias Franklin J. Tolby, https://www.ancestry.com/discoveryui-content/view/546033:4654?tid=&pid=&queryId=32f910f4-535f-4326-863d-cb71e47ac1b4&_phsrc=JdZ19&_phstart=successSource; letter from F. J. Tolby to Elizabeth Ann Fisher, January 29, 1874, New Mexico Annual Conference of The United Methodist Church Archives; 1850 Federal Census for Eel River, Hendricks County, IN: B. Franklin

Tolby; 1860 Federal Census for Tippecanoe Township, Tippecanoe County, IN: James F. Tolby.

2. Thomas Harwood, *History of New Mexico Spanish and English Missions of the Methodist Episcopal Church From 1850 to 1910*, 2 vols. (Albuquerque: El Abogado Press, 1908–10), 1:237.

3. Letter from F. J. Tolby to Elizabeth Ann Fisher, January 29, 1874, New Mexico Annual Conference of the United Methodist Church Archives.

4. Harwood, *History of New Mexico Missions*, 1:236.

5. Letter from F. J. Tolby to Lizzie Louth, April 7, 1874, New Mexico Annual Conference of the United Methodist Church Archives.

6. Morris F. Taylor, "Plains Indians on the New Mexico–Colorado Border: The Last Phase, 1870–1876," *New Mexico Historical Review* 46, no. 4 (1971): 328–29; Michael D. Pierce, "Red River War (1874–1875)," *Oklahoma Historical Society*, accessed 2021, https://www.okhistory.org/publications/enc/entry.php?entry=RE010; James L. Haley, "Red River War," *Handbook of Texas Online*, updated January 27, 2021, https://www.tshaonline.org/handbook/entries/red-river-war; letter from Tolby to Louth, July 29, 1874, New Mexico Annual Conference of the United Methodist Church Archives.

7. Letter from Tolby to Louth, July 29, 1874, New Mexico Annual Conference of the United Methodist Church Archives.

8. "The North-West Indiana Conference Minutes of 1876," 49, New Mexico Annual Conference of the United Methodist Church Archives; Harwood, *History of New Mexico Missions*, 1:262 and 266; Taylor, *O. P. McMains*, 33 and 36; deposition of Springer, August 9, 1878, Angel Report against Axtell, Int. Dept. Appt. Papers; Henry M. Porter, *Pencilings of an Early Western Pioneer* (Denver: World Press, 1929), 28; Caffey, *Frank Springer and New Mexico*, 32.

9. Deposition of Springer, August 9, 1878, Angel Report against Axtell, Int. Dept. Appt. Papers; testimony of O. P. McMains as reported in an undated copy of the *Cimarron News and Press*, Int. Dept. Appt. Papers.

10. Melvin W. Mills vs. William R. Morley, New Mexico Supreme Court Records, January Term, 1876, United States Territorial and New Mexico Supreme Court Records, series 1, Territorial Supreme Court Cases, folder 78, box 8, New Mexico State Records Center and Archives; Kevin McDevitt, with Ed Sitzberger, *History of the St. James Hotel, Cimarron, New Mexico* (Colorado Springs: Cimarron Press, 2019), 43–44; Darlis A. Miller, *Open Range: The Life of*

Agnes Morley Cleaveland (Norman: University of Oklahoma Press, 2010), 5.

11. Lamar, " Santa Fe Ring" in Ellis, *New Mexico, Past and Present*, 155; Cleaveland and Fitzpatrick, *Morleys*, 77; Westphall, *Thomas Benton Catron*, 113.

12. *Santa Fe Daily New Mexican*, September 13, 1875.

13. Agnes Morley Cleaveland, William Morley's daughter, later claimed that Tolby and her father wrote "a series of articles" for the *Sun*; however, it was only a single, anonymous letter, followed by a letter from Simeon H. Newman, that caused the trouble in 1875. The only statement from the time that wasn't simply rumor or suspicion is the *Sun's* denial that Tolby wrote the letter. Cleaveland, *No Life for a Lady*, 7; *New York Sun*, February 7, 1876; deposition of Springer, August 9, 1878, Angel Report against Axtell, Int. Dept. Appt. Papers.

14. Testimony of James Coleman and James Gilchrist, as reported in an undated copy of the *Cimarron News and Press*, Int. Dept. Appt. Papers.

Notes for Chapter 4

1. Testimony of D. W. Stevenson, copied from the *Cimarron News and Press*, Int. Dept. Appt. Papers.

2. Testimony of Mr. Lerhume and S. H. Irwin, copied from the *Cimarron News and Press*, Int. Dept. Appt. Papers; "The North-West Indiana Conference Minutes of 1876," 49, New Mexico Annual Conference of the United Methodist Church Archives; Taulbee, *Taulbee*, 21; *Mesilla News*, September 25, 1875; *Santa Fe Daily New Mexican*, September 18, 1875 and May 1, 1876; *New York Times*, September 20, 1875; deposition of Springer, August 9, 1878, Angel Report against Axtell, Int. Dept. Appt. Papers; 1870 Federal Census for Colfax County, NM: Henry Pascoe.

3. Testimony of S. H. Irwin, copied from the *Cimarron News and Press*, Int. Dept. Appt. Papers; *Santa Fe Daily New Mexican*, September 18, 1875; *New York Times*, November 14, 1875.

4. Testimony of S. H. Irwin, copied from the *Cimarron News and Press*, Int. Dept. Appt. Papers; Bureau of Land Management, General Land Office Records record for Samuel H. Irwin, Issue Data: September 18, 1891, in Colfax County, https://www.ancestry.com/discoveryui-content/view/9387902:1246?tid=&pid=&queryId=a6689f48-4d37-4cf7-a230-bac011eb98be&_phsrc=JdZ88&_phstart=successSource, 1850 Federal

Census for Saline County, MO: Samuel H. Irwin; 1880 Federal Census for Colfax County, NM: Samuel H. Irwin; *Las Vegas Gazette*, November 13, 1875.

5. Testimony of S. H. Irwin, copied from the *Cimarron News and Press*, Int. Dept. Appt. Papers.

6. *Santa Fe Weekly New Mexican*, September 28 and October 12, 1875.

7. Taylor, *O. P. McMains*, 10–13, 14, and 18; 1870 Federal Census for Pueblo, CO: Oscar McMains; Isaac Haight Beardsley, *Echoes from Peak and Plain; or, Tales of Life, War, Travel, and Colorado Methodism* (Cincinnati: Curts & Jennings, 1898), 274–75, 279–80, 283, 291, 320–21, and 345; Ansel Watrous, *History of Larimer County Colorado* (Fort Collins: Courier Printing and Publishing, 1911), 207; *Colorado Daily Chieftain*, September 5 and December 24, 1872.

8. Taylor, *O. P. McMains*, 27–29 and 32; 1880 Federal Census for Colfax County, NM.

9. Taylor, *O. P. McMains*, 38.

10. Harwood, *History of New Mexico Missions*, 1:299 and 2:390.

11. Chuck Parsons, *Clay Allison: Portrait of a Shootist* (Seagraves, TX: Pioneer Book Publishers, 1983), 1–2; Sharon Cunningham, "The Allison Clan: A Visit," *Western-Outlaw Lawman Association Journal* (Winter 2003); copy of Captain Phillips' Company Muster Roll, record for R. A. C. Allison, Chuck Parsons Papers (in author's collection); Roster of Captain J. W. Phillips' Light Artillery Co. TN, www.tnfraziers.com/csa/roster.html.

12. Copy of Certificate of Disability for Discharge, Chuck Parsons Papers.

13. Parsons, *Clay Allison*, 3; "19th (Biffle's) Tennessee Cavalry Regiment," *Tennessee & the Civil War*, November 25, 2016, https://tngenweb.org/civilwar/19th-biffles-tennessee-cavalry-regiment/.

14. *Message of the President of the United States and Accompanying Documents to the Two Houses of Congress at the Commencement of the Third Session of the Fortieth Congress* (Washington, DC: Government Printing Office, 1868), 184–85; Mark V. Wetherington, "Ku Klux Klan," *Tennessee Encyclopedia*, accessed 2022, https://tennesseeencyclopedia.net/entries/ku-klux-klan/.

15. Parsons, *Clay Allison*, 4 and 9–16; Cunningham, "Allison Clan," 17; *Santa Fe Daily New Mexican*, December 30 and 31, 1873, and January 13, 1874; Bill Stockton, "Clifton House," *New Mexico Magazine*, February 1963, 9–10; Frank Clifford, *Deep Trails in the Old West: A Frontier Memoir*, ed. Frederick Nolan (Norman: University

of Oklahoma Press, 2011), 25 and 30; Cleaveland and Fitzpatrick, *Morleys*, 79; Charles Siringo, *Riata and Spurs: The Story of a Lifetime in the Saddle as a Cowboy and Detective* (Boston and New York: Houghton Mifflin, 1931), 176.

16. Parsons, *Clay Allison*, 16; *Colorado Daily Chieftain*, November 3, 1875; *Santa Fe Daily New Mexican*, November 9, 1875; Clifford, *Deep Trails in the Old West*, 30; Cleaveland and Fitzpatrick, *Morleys*, 83; George E. Crocker, "Memories of Cimarron, New Mexico, 1871–1882" (unpublished manuscript), Virginia Beach Public Library System.

17. Testimony of S. H. Irwin and James Gilchrist, copied from the *Cimarron News and Press*, Int. Dept. Appt. Papers; deposition of Springer, August 9, 1878, Angel Report against Axtell, Int. Dept. Appt. Papers; 1880 Federal Census for Colfax County, NM: Andrew J. Howell.

18. *Cimarron News and Press*, August 30, 1877; *Santa Fe Daily New Mexican*, August 28, 1877.

19. *Cimarron News and Press*, August 30, 1877; *Santa Fe Daily New Mexican*, August 28, 1877; testimony of William Low, Isaiah Rinehart, Irvin W. Lacy, and S. Erastus Welding, as reported in an undated copy of the *Cimarron News and Press*, Int. Dept. Appt. Papers; *Colorado Daily Chieftain*, November 3, 1875; Cleaveland and Fitzpatrick, *Morleys*, 100; Clifford, *Deep Trails in the Old West*, 27–28.

20. *Cimarron News and Press*, August 30, 1877; *Santa Fe Daily New Mexican*, August 28, 1877; testimony of William Low and Irvin W. Lacy, as reported in an undated copy of the *Cimarron News and Press*, Int. Dept. Appt. Papers; 1870 Federal Census for Colfax County, NM: Simon [*sic*] E Welding; Charles Bent, ed., *History of Whiteside County, Illinois, From its First Settlement to the Present Time* (Clinton, IA: L. P. Allen, Printer and Binder, 1877), 358; *Colorado Daily Chieftain*, November 3, 1875; Cleaveland and Fitzpatrick, *Morleys*, 100; Clifford, *Deep Trails in the Old West*, 27–28.

Notes for Chapter 5

1. Santa Fe *New Mexican*, November 5, 1875; *Colorado Daily Chieftain*, November 3, 1875; Cleaveland and Fitzpatrick, *Morleys*, 101; Clifford, *Deep Trails in the Old West*, 31–32; deposition of Springer, August 9, 1878, Angel Report against Axtell, Int. Dept. Appt. Papers; copy of undated article from the *Cimarron News and Press*, Int. Dept. Apt. Papers; Parsons, *Clay Allison*, 21.

2. *Santa Fe Daily New Mexican*, November 5, 1875; drawings of St. James Hotel barroom interior by Fred Lambert, Fred Lambert Papers, MSS 519 BC, box 1, folder 1, Center for Southwest Research, UNM.

3. Ada Morley's notes as quoted in Cleaveland and Fitzpatrick, *Morleys*, 101–2; Miller, *Open Range*, 6–7.

4. Undated recollection in the William G. Ritch Collection, RI 1742, Huntington Library.

5. Cleaveland and Fitzpatrick, *Morleys*, 101–2; *Colorado Daily Chieftain*, November 10, 1875; deposition of Springer, August 9, 1878, Angel Report against Axtell, Int. Dept. Appt. Papers; copy of undated article from the *Cimarron News and Press*, Int. Dept. Appt. Papers; Recko, "Axtell's 'Dear Ben' Letter," 43–44; Harwood, *History of New Mexico Missions*, 1:266.

6. Statement of Manuel Cardenas, as reported in a copy of undated article from the *Cimarron News and Press*, Int. Dept. Appt. Papers.

7. Harwood, *History of New Mexico Missions*, 1:266–69; M. W. Mills to C. N. Blackwell, February 13, 1924, copy in the collection of Ed Gooden, Albuquerque, NM.

8. Deposition of Springer, August 9, 1878, Angel Report against Axtell, Int. Dept. Appt. Papers.

9. Affidavit of William R. Morley, June 15, 1878, Frank Springer Papers, CS Cattle Company, Cimarron, NM (hereafter cited as Frank Springer Papers).

10. Parsons, *Clay Allison*, 21; deposition of Springer, August 9, 1878, Angel Report against Axtell, Int. Dept. Appt. Papers; Cleaveland and Fitzpatrick, *Morleys*, 101; copy of undated article from the *Cimarron News and Press*, Int. Dept. Appt. Papers; *Santa Fe Daily New Mexican*, November 9 and 10, 1875; David L. Caffey, *When Cimarron Meant Wild: The Maxwell Land Grant Conflict in New Mexico and Colorado* (Norman: University of Oklahoma Press, 2023), 102. Many years later Melvin Mills claimed that when he arrived in Cimarron Plaza by coach to face the charges against him, an angry mob of armed men pulled him from his coach and were about to hang him when friends of his intervened. There's no contemporary account to back up Mills's claim; see Mills to Blackwell, February 13, 1924, copy in the collection of Ed Gooden.

11. *Santa Fe Daily New Mexican*, November 9 and 10, 1875; Cleaveland and Fitzpatrick, *Morleys*, 101–2; *Colorado Daily Chieftain*, November 10, 1875; copy of undated article from the *Cimarron News and Press*,

Int. Dept. Appt. Papers; deposition of Springer, August 9, 1878, Angel Report against Axtell, Int. Dept. Appt. Papers; Caffey, *When Cimarron Meant Wild*, 103.

12. Copy of undated article from the *Cimarron News and Press*, Int. Dept. Appt. Papers.

13. Copy of undated article from the *Cimarron News and Press*, Int. Dept. Appt. Papers; *Santa Fe Daily New Mexican*, November 15, 1875; *Colorado Daily Chieftain*, November 12, 1875.

14. Testimony of I. Rinehart, Jules Howard, Joseph Herberger, Alexander Dull, and Mr. Wooley as reported in a copy of undated article from the *Cimarron News and Press*, Int. Dept. Appt. Papers.

15. Testimony of R. C. Allison, Joseph Curtis, and Jules Howard, as reported in a copy of undated article from the *Cimarron News and Press*, Int. Dept. Appt. Papers.

16. Testimony of I. W. Lacy as reported in a copy of undated article from the *Cimarron News and Press*, Int. Dept. Appt. Papers.

17. Testimony of R. C. Allison as reported in a copy of undated article from the *Cimarron News and Press*, Int. Dept. Appt. Papers.

18. Testimony of Jules Howard as reported in a copy of undated article from the *Cimarron News and Press*, Int. Dept. Appt. Papers.

19. Testimony of Mr. Tison as reported in a copy of undated article from the *Cimarron News and Press*, Int. Dept. Appt. Papers.

20. Testimony of M. W. Mills as reported in a copy of undated article from the *Cimarron News and Press*, Int. Dept. Appt. Papers.

21. Testimony of Florencio Donoghue as reported in a copy of undated article from the *Cimarron News and Press*, Int. Dept. Appt. Papers.

22. Copy of undated article from the *Cimarron News and Press*, Int. Dept. Appt. Papers.

23. Copy of undated article from the *Cimarron News and Press*, Int. Dept. Appt. Papers; *Colorado Daily Chieftain*, November 12, 1875; Oliva, *Fort Union*, 396.

24. Recko, " Axtell's 'Dear Ben' Letter," 44; deposition of Springer, August 9, 1878, Angel Report against Axtell, Int. Dept. Appt. Papers; Clifford, *Deep Trails in the Old West*, 28; Crocker, "Memories of Cimarron."

25. Along with McMains as chairman, the following people were elected as vice presidents for the meeting: Mathew Lynch, Irvin Lacy, Peter Burleson, and Samuel Irwin; copy of undated article from the *Cimarron News and Press*, Int. Dept. Appt. Papers; 1870 Federal Census

for Stephenville, TX: Irvin W. Lacy; 1880 Federal Census for Colfax
County, New Mexico: I. W. Lacy.

26. Copy of undated article from the *Cimarron News and Press*, Int. Dept.
Appt. Papers.

27. Copy of undated article from the *Cimarron News and Press*, Int. Dept.
Appt. Papers.

28. *Las Vegas Gazette*, November 13, 1875; *Western Christian Advocate*, November 17, 1875.

Notes for Chapter 6

1. *Santa Fe Daily New Mexican*, December 21, 1875; Caffey, *Chasing the Santa Fe Ring*, 244–45.

2. "Territory of Elkins," *New York Sun*, December 16, 1875.

3. Copy of the *Cimarron News and Press*, December 31, 1875, Int. Dept. Appt. Papers.

4. Copy of the *Cimarron News and Press*, December 31, 1875, Int. Dept. Appt. Papers; Frank M. O'Brien, *The Story of The Sun* (New York: George H. Doran Company, 1918), 425.

5. *Cimarron News and Press*, February 18, 1876. The men who signed the letter were George Thompson, John Faulkney, J. A. Herberger, G. T. Peter, Thomas Clouser, F. J. Will, Joseph Lowrey, Michael Kelly, S. H. Irwin, E. S. Mead, William M. King, Thomas Knott, Alonzo Service, Jack Riley, S. W. Richmond, John Cossairt, David Verner, W. S. Mulhern, D. Beal, Thomas Bird, Thomas Ritchey, A. McKinsey, H. West, A. Holmes, H. Rankin, S. W. Lane, Charles Rand, John Irwin, Joe [John?] G. Chichester, Lewis W. Coe, N. D. Brown, George B. Foster, George W. Cook, A. A. Maxwell, John A. Maxwell, H. D. Thacker, E. C. Brown, John Thacker, Benjamin F. Scott, Byron Codlin, Robert E. Gray, John Burr, James Marr, William Walker, Will J. Grandstaff, John T. Bates, A. M. Coe, J. W. Coe, L. McD. Smith, James Finch, John Gates, B. F. Houx, Frank Alexander, George Croxford, Warren Hewett, Orange Phelps, Henry Lambert, John Lee, H. Schwenk, Richard Steel, Allen H. Carey, B. Chandler, John Walters, Sinclair W. Wightman, H. W. Ellington, Robert Stepp, William A. Crocker, Z. McFadden, James E. Temple, George Hitchings, L. Hudson, George Milner, W. H. Newton, John Caton, John E. Codlin, William Morley, Frank Springer, D. W. Stevens, C. N. Storey, J. F. Sanders, Aaron Hollenbeck, H. H. Holford, W. W. Boilenger, Edward Collins, G. W. Smith, D. Cummings, E. L.

Reynolds, W. A. Bearce, G. Turner, Patrick Cullen, George H. Buck, George W. Willison, S. G. Horner, Charles Nihart, John Montgomery, B. C. Keep, George M. Carpenter, William Middleton, Judd Ritter, W. K. Irwin, T. Meloch, M. M. Chase, Will Terhune, O. P. McMains, Peter Burleson, R. C. Allison, C. H. Hoodman, John Gilbert, J. W. Allison, John Hefferen, David Crockett, James N. Cook, E. D. Willis, J. W. Bohannon, D. L. Wilson, William Gravelle, H. V. Graves, Abram Sever, G. W. Morrison, William L. Goodlett, Z. A. Curtis, J. Cox, J. W. Curtis, T. H. Curtis, Isaac Denby, C. H. Bartlett, George W. Geer, William Woolley, William Weev, A. H. Lawrence, C. A. Marsland, Frank Coe, J. E. Grace, J. O. Cunningham, O. K. Chittenden, H. M. Porter, B. D. Barnes, T. J. Monaghan, N. Mitchel, W. H. Wilcox, James A. Coleman, T. Henderson, E. H. Bergmann, G. A. Bushnell, S. M. Beardsley, Harry Whigham, Matt Crosby, John M. Shafer, Lower Hale, John Hale, Joshua Hale, J. B. Dawson, and W. E. Corbett.

6. Caffey, *Frank Springer and New Mexico*, 36; *Cimarron News and Press*, January 7, 1876.

7. *Cimarron News and Press*, January 7, 1876.

8. *Message of Gov. Samuel B. Axtell to the Legislative Assembly of New Mexico, Twenty-second Session* (Santa Fe, NM: Manderfield & Tucker, Public Printers, 1875).

9. *Santa Fe Daily New Mexican*, January 17, 1876.

10. *Santa Fe Daily New Mexican*, January 17, 1876; depositions of Springer, June 10, 1878, and August 13, 1878, Int. Dept. Appt. Papers; *Mesilla News*, January 29, 1876; Recko, "Axtell's 'Dear Ben' Letter," 44.

11. *Mesilla News*, January 29, 1876.

12. Cleaveland and Fitzpatrick, *Morleys*, 114; *Mesilla News*, January 29, 1876; *Raton Daily Range*, July 22, 1887; Clifford, *Deep Trails in the Old West*, 29; Crocker, Memories of Cimarron"; Porter, *Pencilings*, 29.

13. Cleaveland, *No Life for a Lady*, 8; Cleaveland and Fitzpatrick, *Morleys*, 114–15.

14. Cleaveland, *No Life for a Lady*, 8.

15. Cleaveland and Fitzpatrick, *Morleys*, 82–83; Miller, *Open Range*, 3.

Notes for Chapter 7

1. *Cimarron News and Press*, January 28, 1876.

2. *Cimarron News and Press*, January 28, 1876, February 11, 1876; the *News and Press* reported, "We had a streak of luck in finding that the old press

of the Cimarron *News* office, which was burned in 1871, was similar to the one recently smashed. By taking parts of each we have got a new press, except one piece, which will arrive by express, we hope, in time for us to get out next week's paper. We shall then resume our old size and try to make the paper better than ever."

3. *Mesilla News*, January 29, 1876; Larry Ball, *Desert Lawmen: The High Sheriffs of New Mexico and Arizona Territories, 1846–1912* (Albuquerque: University of New Mexico Press, 1992), 356; O. K. Chittenden to Frank Springer, September 26, 1876, Frank Springer Papers; *History of New Mexico*, 1:270.

4. Axtell to Ulysses S. Grant, January 22, 1876, as quoted in John T. Simon, ed., *The Papers of Ulysses S. Grant*, vol. 27 (Carbondale: Southern Illinois University Press, 2005), 356.

5. Deposition of Springer, August 13, 1878, Int. Dept. Appt. Papers.

6. Deposition of Springer, August 13, 1878, Int. Dept. Appt. Papers; deposition of Springer, August 9, 1878, Angel Report against Axtell, and deposition of Springer, June 10, 1878, Int. Dept. Appt. Papers; *Cimarron News and Press*, April 18, 1878.

7. Deposition of Springer, August 9, 1878, Angel Report against Axtell, and deposition of Springer, June 10, 1878, and deposition of William R. Morley, May 30, 1878, Int. Dept. Appt. Papers.

8. Deposition of Morley, May 30, 1878, Int. Dept. Appt. Papers.

9. Deposition of Morley, May 30, 1878, Int. Dept. Appt. Papers; deposition of Springer, August 9, 1878, Angel Report against Axtell, Int. Dept. Appt. Papers; *Cimarron News and Press*, August 9, 1878; Moore, Francis, to the commanding officer, March 25, 1876, Letters Received by Headquarters, District of New Mexico, September 1865–August 1890, M1088, NARA (hereafter cited as Letters Received by Headquarters).

10. Deposition of Morley, May 30, 1878, Int. Dept. Appt. Papers.

11. Deposition of Morley, May 30, 1878, Int. Dept. Appt. Papers; Springer to Axtell, April 9, 1878, in Angel Report against Axtell, Int. Dept. Appt. Papers.

12. Deposition of Springer, June 10, 1878, Int. Dept. Appt. Papers; *Santa Fe Daily New Mexican*, March 30, 1876.

13. Francis Moore to the A. A. A. General, April 2, 1876, Letters Received by Headquarters.

14. *Santa Fe Daily New Mexican*, March 25, 1876; Chuck Hornung, "The Forgotten Davy Crockett," *Quarterly of the National Asso-*

ciation and Center for Outlaw and Lawman History 13, no. 1
(Summer 1988): 13, and 13, no. 2 (Fall 1988): 14; Parsons, *Clay
Allison*, 25; Registers of Deaths in the Regular Army, 1860–1889,
entries for George Small, John Hanson, and Anthony Harvey,
accessed 2018, https://www.ancestry.com/discoveryui-content/
view/38145:2128?tid=&pid=&queryId=726000a3-20c4-43a7-
9da5-fed214466ad8&_phsrc=JdZ96&_phstart=successSource and
https://www.ancestry.com/discoveryui-content/view/38524:2128?
tid=&pid=&queryId=5d3e2960-1550-4e36-a0cc-89dfe99d22fb&
_phsrc=JdZ93&phstart=successSource; Clifford, *Deep Trails in
the Old West*, 55; Francis Moore to the commanding officer, March
25, 1876, Letters Received by Headquarters.

Notes for Chapter 8

1. *Acts of the Legislative Assembly of the Territory of New Mexico*, Twenty-Second Session (Santa Fe: Manderfield & Tucker, Public Printers,
1876), 16; Caffey, *Chasing the Santa Fe Ring*, 49 and 250.
2. Axtell to General Edward Hatch, March 28, 1876, Letters Received by
Headquarters; *Santa Fe Daily New Mexican*, May 1, 1876.
3. *Santa Fe Daily New Mexican*, May 1, 1876.
4. Parsons, *Clay Allison*, 15–16 and 29; *Santa Fe Daily New Mexican*,
January 13, 1874; deposition of Frank Springer, August 13, 1878, Int.
Dept. Appt. Papers; *Colorado Daily Chieftain*, May 20, 1876; Harwood,
History of New Mexico Missions, 1:302; Taylor, *O. P. McMains*, 50.
5. *Santa Fe Weekly New Mexican*, May 16, 1876.
6. Harwood, *History of New Mexico Missions*, Volume 1:300–301 and
2:390.
7. Taylor, *O. P. McMains*, 50.
8. Taylor, *O. P. McMains*, 50; *Santa Fe Daily New Mexican*, May 26, 27,
and 29, 1876; *Santa Fe Weekly New Mexican*, May 30, 1876.
9. Harwood, *History of New Mexico Missions*, 1:302; Cleaveland and
Fitzpatrick, *Morleys*, 124–25 and 159; Taylor, *O. P. McMains*, 50–51;
Miller, *Open Range*, 7–8; *Proceedings of the American Society of Civil
Engineers* vol. 9 (January–December 1883): 122–23.
10. Deposition of Springer, August 9, 1878, Angel Report against Axtell,
Int. Dept. Appt. Papers.
11. Undated newspaper clipping, Angel Report against Axtell, Int. Dept.
Appt. Papers.

12. Deposition of William D. Lee, August 30, 1877, Int. Dept. Appt. Papers.
13. Hornung, " Forgotten Davy Crockett," *Outlaw and Lawman History* 13, no. 1 (Summer 1988): 13, and 13, no. 2 (Fall 1988): 14; *Santa Fe Daily New Mexican*, September 13, 1876.
14. *Santa Fe Daily New Mexican*, October 10, 1876.
15. Clifford, *Deep Trails in the Old West*, 36.
16. Clifford, *Deep Trails in the Old West*, 36; *Santa Fe Daily New Mexican*, October 4 and 10, 1876; Parsons, *Clay Allison*, 25.

Notes for Chapter 9

1. Cleaveland and Fitzpatrick, *Morleys*, 125–26; Caffey, *Frank Springer and New Mexico*, 16; *Transcript of Title of the Maxwell Land Grant*, 40; McMains to McPherson, February 20, 1877, Int. Dept. Appt. Papers.
2. *Colorado Daily Chieftain*, December 27, 1876.
3. Harry E. Kelsey Jr., "Clay Allison: Western Gunman," chap. 16 in *1957 Brand Book of Denver Westerners* ed. Westerners Denver Posse (Boulder: Johnson), 397–401; *Las Animas Leader*, December 22, 1876; *Colorado Daily Chieftain*, December 27, 1876, and January 3, 1877; Parsons, *Clay Allison*, 30.
4. Parsons, *Clay Allison*, 30–32; *Las Animas Leader*, December 22, 1876, and January 5, 1877; *Colorado Daily Chieftain*, December 31, 1876, and January 9, 1877; Kelsey, "Clay Allison," 400–402; *History of the Arkansas Valley, Colorado, Illustrated* (Chicago: O. L. Baskin and Co., Historical Publishers, 1881), 795.
5. Kelsey, "Clay Allison," 402; Cunningham, "Clay Allison."
6. Emma Hunt to Mary McPherson, February 28, 1877, Int. Dept. Appt. Papers.
7. W. R. Morley to McPherson, March 6, 1877, Int. Dept. Appt. Papers.
8. Ada Morley to McPherson, March 7, 1877, Int. Dept. Appt. Papers.
9. W. B. Matchett and McPherson to the secretary of the interior, March 1877, Int. Dept. Appt. Papers.
10. Matchett and McPherson to the secretary of the interior, March 1877, Int. Dept. Appt. Papers.
11. Charles M. Howard to Matchett, June 9, 1877, Brigham Young to Carl Schurz, July 13, 1877, and Samuel B. Axtell to Carl Schurz, June 14, 1877, Int. Dept. Appt. Papers.
12. Matchett and McPherson to the secretary of the interior, March 1877, Int. Dept. Appt. Papers.

13. *Santa Fe Daily New Mexican*, April 2, 1877; "Solicitor General: Samuel F. Phillips," *Office of the Solicitor General: US Department of Justice*, updated September 19, 2023, https://www.justice.gov/osg/bio/samuel-f-phillips.

Notes for Chapter 10

1. S. B. Axtell to Carl Schurz, May 20, 1877, Int. Dept. Appt. Papers.
2. Axtell to Schurz, June 14, 1877, Int. Dept. Appt. Papers.
3. Stephen B. Elkins to Rutherford B. Hayes, June 11, 1877, Int. Dept. Appt. Papers.
4. Willi Spiegelberg to R. C. McCormick, July 25, 1877, William Breeden to McCormick, August 15, 1877, and Charles Lesinsky to McCormick, August 15, 1877, Int. Dept. Appt. Papers.
5. Deposition of Springer, August 9, 1878, Angel Report against Axtell, and deposition of Harry Whigham, August 15, 1877, Int. Dept. Appt. Papers; Caffey, *Frank Springer and New Mexico*, 42.
6. Newspaper clipping, written by Axtell, that he submitted as a response to charges against him, Angel Report against Axtell, Int. Dept. Appt. Papers.
7. W. B. Matchett and M. E. McPherson to the secretary of the interior, July 26, 1877, Int. Dept. Appt. Papers.
8. Deposition of Lewis Kingman, July 31, 1877, Int. Dept. Appt. Papers; Mari Grana, *On the Fringes of Power: The Life and Turbulent Career of Stephen Wallace Dorsey* (Guilford, CT: Twodot, 2015), 4; Caffey, *Chasing the Santa Fe Ring*, 125; Allen Thorndike Rice, ed., *The North American Review* (New York: North American Review, 1887), 684.
9. Deposition of John L. Taylor, August 6, 1877, Int. Dept. Appt. Papers.
10. *Las Vegas Gazette*, June 30, 1885; Montoya, *Translating Property*, 114; Westphall, *Thomas Benton Catron*, 110; Caffey, *Chasing the Santa Fe Ring*, 51.
11. Montoya, *Translating Property*, 114 and 115–16; Cleaveland and Fitzpatrick, *Morleys*, 87–88; Westphall, *Thomas Benton Catron*, 110; *Report of the Secretary of the Interior; Being Part of the Message and Documents Communicated to the Two Houses of Congress at the Beginning of the First Session of the Forty-Ninth Congress*, vol. 1 (Washington, DC: Government Printing Office, 1885), 283.

Notes for Chapter 11

1. Taylor, *O. P. McMains*, 54.
2. *Cimarron News and Press*, August 30, 1877.
3. *Cimarron News and Press*, August 30, 1877.
4. *Cimarron News and Press*, August 30, 1877.
5. *Cimarron News and Press*, August 30, 1877.
6. *Cimarron News and Press*, August 30, 1877.
7. *Cimarron News and Press*, August 30, 1877.
8. *Cimarron News and Press*, August 30, 1877.
9. Colorado *Weekly Chieftain*, September 6, 1877; *Compiled Laws of New Mexico in Accordance with an Act of the Legislature, Approved April 3, 1884* (Santa Fe: New Mexican Printing Company, Printers and Binders, 1885), 398. Under New Mexico law, murder in the fifth degree was "every other killing of a human being in any other manner, by the act, procurement or culpable negligence of another, where such killing is not justifiable or excusable, or is not declared in this chapter murder of one of the degrees [one through four] already defined, shall be deemed murder in the fifth degree."
10. Taylor, *O. P. McMains*, 55; Arie Poldervaart, "Black-Robed Justice in New Mexico, 1846–1912," *New Mexico Historical Review* 22, no. 4 (1947): 352; *Las Vegas Gazette*, April 6, 1878.
11. David Burleson and Jim Burleson, *The Man Who Tamed Cimarron: The Wild and Unruly Life of Pete Burleson* (North Haven, CT: Burleson Heritage, 2021), 48.
12. Raymond Morley to Ada Morley, September 26, 1877, as quoted in Cleaveland and Fitzpatrick, *Morleys*, 139–41.
13. W. B. Matchett to William Morley, November 21, 1877, as quoted in Cleaveland and Fitzpatrick, *Morleys*, 143–45.

Notes for Chapter 12

1. *Cimarron News and Press*, January 17, 1878.
2. Nolan, *Lincoln County War*, 127, 192, 202, 508, and 510; Nolan, *The West of Billy the Kid* (Norman: University of Oklahoma Press, 1998), 103, 104–5, 111–14, and 115; Robert M. Utley, *High Noon in Lincoln: Violence on the Western Frontier* (Albuquerque: University of New Mexico Press, 1987), 28, 30, 44, 47–49, 54, 56, 58, and 59; Mills, James B., *Billy the Kid: El Bandido Simpático* (Denton: University of North Texas Press, 2022), 169–70 and 174–75.

3. One example is Montague Leverson to Rutherford B. Hayes, April 1, 1878, Frank W. Angel Report on the Death of John H. Tunstall, General Records of the Department of Justice, RG 60, 44-4-8-3, NARA (hereafter cited as Angel Report on Tunstall).

4. Cleaveland and Fitzpatrick, *Morleys*, 149; Victor Westphall, "Colfax County War," 16, manuscript in Audrey Alpers Papers, RG 2001-032, box 15, folder "Morley's Colfax County War," New Mexico State University Archives and Special Collections, Las Cruces, NM; deposition of Springer, August 9, 1878, Angel Report against Axtell, and deposition of Morley, May 30, 1878, Int. Dept. Appt. Papers.

5. Cimarron *New and Press*, April 18, 1878; deposition of Springer, June 10, 1878, Int. Dept. Appt. Papers; Recko, "Axtell's 'Dear Ben' Letter," 45.

6. Springer to Axtell, April 4, 1878, in Angel Report against Axtell, Int. Dept. Appt. Papers.

7. Axtell to Springer, April 7, 1878, in Angel Report against Axtell, Int. Dept. Appt. Papers.

8. Springer to Axtell, April 9, 1878, in Angel Report against Axtell, Int. Dept. Appt. Papers.

9. Axtell to Springer, April 11, 1878, in Angel Report against Axtell, Int. Dept. Appt. Papers.

10. Springer to Axtell, April 18, 1878, in Angel Report against Axtell, Int. Dept. Appt. Papers.

11. *Cimarron News and Press*, April 18, 1878.

12. Axtell to Springer, May 13, 1878, in Angel Report against Axtell, Int. Dept. Appt. Papers.

13. *Cimarron News and Press*, April 18, 1878.

14. *Cimarron News and Press*, May 23, 1878.

15. Springer to Carl Schurz, June 10, 1878; deposition of Springer, June 10, 1878, and deposition of Morley, May 30, 1878, Int. Dept. Appt. Papers.

16. Caffey, *Frank Springer and New Mexico*, 5 and 44; A. Delahaye to Schurz, July 3, 1878, and W. B. Allison to President Hayes, July 4, 1878, Int. Dept. Appt. Papers.

Notes for Chapter 13

1. Frank Angel's office was at 62 Liberty Street, New York: *City College Quarterly* 2, no. 1 (March 1906): 152–53; Nolan, *Lincoln County War*, 442; Sydney C. Van Nort, *The City College of New York* (Charleston: Arcadia, 2007), 18; *University of the State of New*

York: Eighty-Second Annual Report of the Regents of the University (Albany: Argus Company, Printers, 1869), 264; *Trow's New York City Directory, Volume XCII, for the Year Ending May 1, 1879* (New York: Trow City Directory, 1879), 41; 1880 Federal Census for Brooklyn, Kings County, NY: F. Warner Angel.

2. *Santa Fe Weekly New Mexican*, May 4, 1878; Recko, "Axtell's 'Dear Ben' Letter," 50; Frank W. Angel, "In the matter of the examination of charges against Dr. B. M. Thomas U. S. Indian Agent Pueblo Indians of New Mexico, Report" and "In the matter of the Examination of the charges against C. F. [*sic*] Godfroy U. S. Indian Agent Mescalero Apaches N. M., Report," Bureau of Indian Affairs Letters Received, RG 75, M 234, Roll 573, NARA; S. B. Elkins to Charles Devens, September 13, 1878, and T. B. Catron to Charles Devens, September 17, 1878, Angel Report on Tunstall; Angel Report against Axtell, Int. Dept. Appt. Papers; *City College Quarterly* 2, no. 1 (March 1906): 152; Norman Cleaveland, "The Great New Mexico Cover-Up: Frank Warner Angel's Reports," *Outlaw Gazette*, November 2000, 16; Mills, *Billy the Kid*, 214; Altenbrandt, ed., *Men behind the Gins in the Making of Greater Grand Rapids* (Grand Rapids: Dean-Hicks Printing Company, 1909), 196–97; Sharon K. Lowry, "Portrait of an Age: The Political Career of Stephen W. Dorsey, 1868–1899" (PhD diss., University of North Texas, 1980), https://digital.library.unt.edu/ark:/67531/metadc332211/m2/1/high_res_d/1002783254-Lowry.pdf.

3. Utley, *High Noon in Lincoln*, 75; Westphall, *Thomas Benton Catron*, 126.

4. Nolan, *Billy the Kid*, 115 and 143–44; Utley, *High Noon in Lincoln*, 118; Westphall, *Thomas Benton Catron*, 127.

5. S. B. Axtell to President Hayes, July 17, 1878, Int. Dept. Appt. Papers.

6. Utley, *High Noon in Lincoln*, 92 and 104.

7. Deposition of William R. Morley, May 30, 1878, Int. Dept. Appt. Papers; deposition of Morley, June 15, 1878, Frank Springer Papers.

8. Cleaveland and Fitzpatrick, *Morleys*, 152 and 193; *Mesilla News*, June 29, 1878; deposition of Springer, August 9, 1878, Angel Report against Axtell, Int. Dept. Appt. Papers.

9. Deposition of Springer, August 9, 1878, Angel Report against Axtell, Int. Dept. Appt. Papers.

10. Deposition of Springer, August 9, 1878, Angel Report against Axtell, Int. Dept. Appt. Papers.

11. Deposition of Springer, August 9, 1878, Angel Report against Axtell, Int. Dept. Appt. Papers.

12. Deposition of Springer, August 9, 1878, Angel Report against Axtell, Int. Dept. Appt. Papers.
13. Axtell to Frank Warner Angel, August 12, 1878, Angel Report against Axtell, Int. Dept. Appt. Papers.
14. Axtell to C. P. Huntington, August 12, 1878, Collis Potter Huntington Papers, box 26, Special Collections Research Center, Syracuse University Library, Syracuse, NY (hereafter cited as Collis Potter Huntington Papers).
15. Angel to Axtell, August 12, 1878, Angel Report against Axtell, Int. Dept. Appt. Papers.
16. Angel to Carl Schurz, August 24, 1878, Angel Report against Axtell, Int. Dept. Appt. Papers.
17. Copy of letter from Schurz to Hayes, August 31, 1878, Miscellaneous Manuscripts, Rutherford B. Hayes Presidential Center.

Notes for Chapter 14

1. Recko, "Axtell's 'Dear Ben' Letter," 46.
2. *Cimarron News and Press*, September 6, 1878.
3. William Morley to Ada Morley, September 8, 1878, as quoted in Cleaveland and Fitzpatrick, *Morleys*, 158.
4. *Santa Fe Weekly New Mexican*, September 14, 1878.
5. *Santa Fe Weekly New Mexican*, September 21, 1878; Frank Warner Angel to Carl Schurz, October 3, 1878, and attached newspaper clipping, Angel Report against Axtell, Int. Dept. Appt. Papers.
6. S. B. Axtell to C. P. Huntington, September 19, 1878, Collis Potter Huntington Papers.
7. Axtell to Huntington, September 19, 1878, Collis Potter Huntington Papers.
8. Axtell to Huntington, September 19, 1878, Collis Potter Huntington Papers.
9. Axtell to Huntington, September 19, 1878, Collis Potter Huntington Papers.
10. Axtell to Huntington, September 19, 1878, Collis Potter Huntington Papers.
11. Angel to Schurz, October 3, 1878, Angel Report against Axtell, Int. Dept. Appt. Papers.
12. Springer to Schurz, June 10, 1878, Int. Dept. Appt. Papers.

13. "Union Major General Lew Wallace," *National Park Service: Mono-cacy National Battlefield, Maryland*, updated August 26, 2021, www.nps.gov/mono/historyculture/lewwallace.htm; Nolan, *Lincoln County War*, 349 and 490–91.

Notes for Chapter 15

1. Keleher, *Violence in Lincoln County*, 165; Caffey, *Frank Springer and New Mexico*, 46; Lew Wallace to Carl Schurz, October 1, 1878, and Lew Wallace to Sue Wallace, October 8, 1878, the Papers of Lew and Susan Wallace, collection M292, box 3, folder 15, William H. Smith Memorial Library, Indiana Historical Society, Indianapolis, IN (hereafter cited as Papers of Lew and Susan Wallace).

2. Lew Wallace to Schurz, October 1, 1878, and Lew Wallace to Sue Wallace, October 8, 1878, Papers of Lew and Susan Wallace.

3. Lew Wallace to Sue Wallace, October 8, 1878, Papers of Lew and Susan Wallace.

4. Lew Wallace to Ab Markland, November 14, 1878, Papers of Lew and Susan Wallace, series 1, microfilm reel 13.

5. "Axtell, Samuel Beach," in Garraty and Carnes, *American National Biography* 1:784–86; "Samuel Beach Axtell," *New Mexico History: State Records Center & Archives*, accessed 2018, http://newmexicohistory.org/people/samuel-beach-axtell; Keleher, *Violence in Lincoln County*, 29–30; *Summit County Beacon*, March 23, 1881; William Henry Perrin, ed., *History of Summit County, with an Outline Sketch of Ohio* (Chicago: Baskin & Battey, Historical Publishers, 1881), 997.

6. *City College Quarterly* 2, no. 1 (March 1906): 153.

7. Westphall, *Thomas Benton Catron*, 133; Cleaveland, "Great New Mexico Cover-Up," 16; "Catron, Thomas Benton"; S. B. Elkins to Charles Devens, September 13, 1878, and T. B. Catron to Charles Devens, September 17, 1878, Angel Report on Tunstall; "Former Mayors of Santa Fe," accessed 2014, https://santafenm.gov/elected-officials/mayors-of-santa-fe.

8. Nolan, *Lincoln County War*, 459; "Elkins, Stephen Benton"; http://historicelkins.com; "D&E History," accessed 2014, https://www.dewv.edu/about/mission-vision-history/; Caffey, *Chasing the Santa Fe Ring*, 91.

9. *Santa Fe Daily New Mexican*, March 1, 1895; *Albuquerque Journal*, August 20, 1925; Franklin Harper, ed., *Who's Who on the Pacific Coast*

(Los Angeles: Harper, 1913), 402; Lansing B. Bloom and Paul A. F. Walter, eds., *The New Mexico Historical Review* (Santa Fe: Historical Society of New Mexico, 1926), 1:86–87.

10. Cleaveland and Fitzpatrick, *Morleys*, 193, 214, and 219; *Las Vegas Gazette*, January 4, 1883.

11. Miller, *Open Range*, 16, 28–29; Ancestry.com page for Ada McPherson by Abedichek, https://www.ancestry.com/family-tree/person/ tree/68763515/person/212058489982/facts; Cleaveland and Fitzpatrick, *Morleys*, 219.

12. *Boston Globe*, Wednesday, September 8, 1897.

13. Cleaveland and Fitzpatrick, *Morleys*, 2–3, 224–25, and 234; Miller, *Open Range*, 61; "Ada McPherson Morley," *New Mexico Humanities Council*, accessed 2021, https://nmhumanities.org/NMwomen2020/ SecondarySources/Suffrage%20NM%20Ada%20McPherson%20 Morley.pdf; *Evening Herald* (Albuquerque), December 15, 1917; Joan Jensen, "Disfranchisement Is a Disgrace: Women and Politics in New Mexico, 1900–1940," *New Mexico Historical Review* 56, no. 1 (1981): 5, 17–18; *Hearings Before the Committee on Woman Suffrage, United States Senate, Sixty-Third Congress, First Session on S. J. Res. 1* (Washington, DC: Government Printing Office, 1913), 2; Ancestry.com page for Ada McPherson by Abedichek.

14. Caffey, *Frank Springer and New Mexico*, 19, 53, 55, 56, 62, 94, 98, 137, 144, 197–99, 207; "Springer Echinoderm Collection," *Smithsonian National Museum of National History*, accessed 2020, https:// naturalhistory.si.edu/research/paleobiology/collections-overview/ springer-echinoderm-collection.

15. Caffey, *Frank Springer and New Mexico*, 209–10; Wroth, "Maxwell Land Grant"; "Maxwell Shareholders Approve ABN AMRO, Dresdner Bid (Dutch)," *Bloomberg*, March 17, 2000, https://www.bloomberg.com/press-releases/2000-03-17/maxwell-shareholders-approve-abn-amro-dresdner-bid-dutch.

16. Stephen Zimmer and Gene Lamm, *Images of America: Colfax County* (Charleston, SC: Arcadia, 2015), 7 and 69; Randall M. MacDonald, Gene Lamm, and Sarah E. MacDonald, *Images of America: Cimarron and Philmont* (Charleston, SC: Arcadia, 2012), 8, 41, and 55; "Cimarron," NewMexico.org, accessed 2022, https:// www.newmexico.org/places-to-visit/regions/northeast/cimarron/; "Discover Cimarron, NM," CimarronNM.com, accessed 2022, http://www.cimarronnm.com.

17. Parsons, *Clay Allison*, 43, 44, 45, 47, 51, and 54; Sharon Cunningham, "Clay Allison: Good-Natured Holy Terror," *HistoryNet*, July 30, 2013, www.historynet.com/clay-allison-good-natured-holy-terror.htm; C. L. Sonnichsen, "Allison, Robert Clay (1841–1887)," *Handbook of Texas Online*, updated November 1, 1994, www.tshaonline.org/handbook/online/articles/fal39; Cunningham, "Allison Clan"; Fred Lambert, "Cimarron's Clay Allison Lived the Law of the Gun," *Raton Daily Range*, June 16, 1954.

Notes for Chapter 16

1. Taylor, *O. P. McMains*, 66 and 67–69; Government Accountability Office Report to Congress, June 2004, in *Treaty of Guadalupe Hidalgo, Findings and Possible Options*, 72; Interstate Land Co. v. Maxwell Land Grant Co., April 6, 1891, in *United States Reports*, vol. 139, *Cases Adjudged in the Supreme Court in the October Term, 1890* (New York and Albany: Banks & Brothers, Law Publishers, 1891), 570.
2. Taylor, *O. P. McMains*, 66 and 69.
3. Raymond Morley to Ada Morley, as quoted in Cleaveland and Fitzpatrick, *Morleys*, 206.
4. Taylor, *O. P. McMains*, 71 and 73.
5. Taylor, *O. P. McMains*, 73; "James Garfield," WhiteHouse.gov, accessed 2014, www.whitehouse.gov/1600/presidents/jamesgarfield.
6. Taylor, *O. P. McMains*, 73, 74–75, 78, and 83; "Isaac Wayne MacVeagh (1881): Attorney General," *UVA Miller Center*, accessed 2014, https://millercenter.org/president/arthur/essays/macveagh-1881-attorney-general.
7. Taylor, *O. P. McMains*, 85–86.
8. Taylor, *O. P. McMains*, 92–93 and 94.
9. Taylor, *O. P. McMains*, 97–98 and 104; F. Stanley, *Raton Chronicle* (Raton, NM: Coda, 2006), 83; 1880 Federal Census, Dry Cimarron and Chino, Colfax County, NM: Charles B. Adams.
10. Taylor, *O. P. McMains*, 108–9, 112, and 113; Stanley, *Grant that Maxwell Bought*, 137.
11. Taylor, *O. P. McMains*, 112, 113, and 116; Maxwell Land Grant Case, 121 U.S. 325 (1887), *Justia*, accessed 2015, https://supreme.justia.com/cases/federal/us/121/325/; *Annual Report of the Commissioner of the General Land Office for the Year 1885* (Washington, DC: Government Printing Office, 1885), 121.

12. Taylor, *O. P. McMains*, 121–22, 137, 138–39, 148, and 150; Morris F. Taylor, "The Two Land Grants of Gervacio Nolán," *New Mexico Historical Review* 47, no. 2 (1972): 170–71, 172–73, 174.

13. Maxwell Land Grant Case, 121 U.S. 325 (1887).

14. *Washington Evening Star*, April 2, 1888; *Washington Post*, April 3, 1888.

15. *Washington Evening Star*, April 2, 1888.

16. *Washington Critic*, April 2, 1888.

17. *Washington Evening Star*, April 2, 1888; *Sacramento Daily Record-Union*, April 3, 1888.

18. *Bismarck Weekly Tribune*, April 13, 1888.

19. Taylor, *O. P. McMains*, 202–4 and 208–9.

20. Taylor, *O. P. McMains*, 214, 216, 218, 219–24, 225, 227, and 234; Montoya, *Translating Property*, 194.

21. Taylor, *O. P. McMains*, 212, 214, 216, 230, 232–34, 242–44, and 250; *Colorado Daily Chieftain*, August 26 and 28, 1888; *Aspen Evening Chronicle*, August 27, 1888; *Meeker Herald*, September 1, 1888.

22. Taylor, *O. P. McMains*, 247, 251–54, and 258–60.

23. Taylor, *O. P. McMains*, 267 and 270.

24. Taylor, *O. P. McMains*, 273–75.

Bibliography

Documents

1850 Federal Census for Eel River, Hendricks County, IN.

1850 Federal Census for Hancock, IL.

1850 Federal Census for Saline County, MO.

1855 Massachusetts State Census for Blandford, Hampden County, MA.

1860 Federal Census for Tippecanoe Township, Tippecanoe County, IN.

1860 Federal Census for Township No. 1, County of Amador, CA.

1870 Federal Census for Colfax County, NM.

1870 Federal Census for Pottawattamie, IA.

1870 Federal Census for Pueblo, CO.

1870 Federal Census for Stephenville, TX.

1880 Federal Census for Brooklyn, Kings County, NY.

1880 Federal Census for Colfax County, NM.

1880 Federal Census for Washington, DC.

1888 Federal Census for Colfax County, NM.

Crocker, George E. "Memories of Cimarron, New Mexico, 1871–1882" (unpublished manuscript). Virginia Beach Public Library System, Virginia Beach, VA.

Deaths Registered in the city of Boston in 1897, Mary McPherson. Accessed 2018. https://www.ancestry.com/imageviewer/collections/2101/images/41262_b139436-00362?pId=2217979.

Registers of Deaths in the Regular Army, 1860–1889. Entries for George Small, John Hanson, and Anthony Harvey. Accessed 2018. https://www.ancestry.com/discoveryui-content/view/38145:2128?tid=&pid=&queryId=726000a3-20c4-43a7-9da5-fed214466ad8&_phsrc=JdZ96&_phstart=successSource and https://www.ancestry.com/discoveryui-content/view/38524:2128?tid=&pid=&queryId=5d3e2960-1550-4e36-a0cc-89dfe99d22fb&_phsrc=JdZ93&_phstart=successSource.

Treaty of Guadalupe Hidalgo: Definition and List of Community Land Grants in New Mexico. Washington, DC: United States General Accounting Office, 2001.

Treaty of Guadalupe Hidalgo: Findings and Possible Options Regarding Longstanding Community Land Grant Claims in New Mexico. Washington, DC: United States General Accounting Office, 2004.

Newspapers

Albuquerque Journal
Aspen Evening Chronicle
Bismarck Weekly Tribune
Boston Globe
Cimarron News and Press
Colorado Daily Chieftain
Evening Herald (Albuquerque)
Evening Journal (Jersey City)
Las Animas Leader
Las Vegas Gazette
Meeker Herald
Mesilla News
New York Sun
New York Times
Raton Daily Range
Raton Weekly Independent
Sacramento Daily Record-Union
Salt Lake Daily Tribune
Santa Fe Daily New Mexican
Santa Fe Weekly New Mexican
Summit County Beacon
Washington Critic
Washington Evening Star
Washington Post
Western Christian Advocate (Cincinnati)

Books and Journals

Acts of the Legislative Assembly of the Territory of New Mexico. Twenty-Second Session. Santa Fe: Manderfield & Tucker, Public Printers, 1876.

Altenbrandt, ed. *The Men behind the Gins in the Making of Greater Grand Rapids.* Grand Rapids: Dean-Hicks Printing Company, 1909.

Annual Report of the Commissioner of the General Land Office for the Year 1885. Washington, DC: Government Printing Office, 1885.

Axtell, Ephraim S. *The Axtell Record: Being a Family Record of the Descendants of Maj. Henry Axtell of Mendham, Morris Co., New Jersey, Who Lived from 1738 to 1818.* Morristown, NJ: Jerseyman, 1886.

Ball, Larry. *Desert Lawmen: The High Sheriffs of New Mexico and Arizona Territories, 1846–1912*. Albuquerque: University of New Mexico Press, 1992.

Beardsley, Isaac Haight. *Echoes from Peak and Plain; or, Tales of Life, War, Travel, and Colorado Methodism*. Cincinnati: Curts & Jennings, 1898.

Bent, Charles, ed. *History of Whiteside County, Illinois, From its First Settlement to the Present Time*. Clinton, IA: L. P. Allen, Printer and Binder, 1877.

Bloom, Lansing B., and Paul A. F. Walter, eds. *The New Mexico Historical Review*. Vol. 1. Santa Fe: Historical Society of New Mexico, 1926.

Borneman, Walter R. *Iron Horses: America's Race to Bring the Railroads West*. New York: Back Bay Books / Little, Brown, 2014.

Bunting, Josiah, III. *Ulysses S. Grant*. New York: Times Books, Henry Holt and Company, 2004.

Burleson, David, and Jim Burleson. *The Man Who Tamed Cimarron: The Wild and Unruly Life of Pete Burleson*. North Haven, CT: Burleson Heritage, 2021.

Caffey, David L. *Chasing the Santa Fe Ring: Power and Privilege in Territorial New Mexico*. Albuquerque: University of New Mexico Press, 2014.

Caffey, David L. *Frank Springer and New Mexico: From the Colfax County War to the Emergence of Modern Santa Fe*. College Station: Texas A&M University Press, 2006.

Caffey, David L. *When Cimarron Meant Wild: The Maxwell Land Grant Conflict in New Mexico and Colorado*. Norman: University of Oklahoma Press, 2023.

Chase, C. M. *The Editor's Run in New Mexico and Colorado*. Montpelier, VT: Argus and Patriot Steam Book and Job Printing House, 1882.

Chávez, Thomas E. *An Illustrated History of New Mexico*. Albuquerque: University of New Mexico Press, 1992.

City College Quarterly 2, no. 1 (March 1906).

Cleaveland, Agnes Morley. *No Life for a Lady*. Lincoln: University of Nebraska Press, 1977.

Cleaveland, Norman, and George Fitzpatrick. *The Morleys: Young Upstarts on the Southwest Frontier*. Albuquerque: Calvin Horn, 1971.

Clifford, Frank. *Deep Trails in the Old West: A Frontier Memoir*. Edited by Frederick Nolan. Norman: University of Oklahoma Press, 2011.

Collinson, John. *The Maxwell Land Grant, Situated in Colorado and New Mexico, United States of America*. London: Taylor and Co., 1870.

Compiled Laws of New Mexico in Accordance with an Act of the Legislature, Approved April 3, 1884. Santa Fe: New Mexican Printing Company, Printers and Binders, 1885.

Cooper, Gale. *The Santa Fe Ring Versus Billy the Kid.* Albuquerque: Gelcour Books, 2018.

Ellis, Richard N., ed. *New Mexico, Past and Present: A Historical Reader.* Albuquerque: University of New Mexico Press, 1971.

Etulain, Richard W., ed. *New Mexican Lives: Profiles and Historical Stories.* Albuquerque: University of New Mexico Press, 2002.

Garraty, John A., and Mark C. Carnes, eds. *American National Biography.* 24 vols. New York: Oxford University Press, 1999.

Grana, Mari. *On the Fringes of Power: The Life and Turbulent Career of Stephen Wallace Dorsey.* Guilford, CT: Twodot, 2015.

Harper, Franklin, ed. *Who's Who on the Pacific Coast.* Los Angeles: Harper, 1913.

Harwood, Thomas. *History of New Mexico Spanish and English Missions of the Methodist Episcopal Church From 1850 to 1910.* 2 vols. Albuquerque: El Abogado Press, 1908–10.

Hearings Before the Committee on Woman Suffrage, United States Senate, Sixty-Third Congress, First Session on S. J. Res. 1. Washington, DC: Government Printing Office, 1913.

History of the Arkansas Valley, Colorado, Illustrated. Chicago: O. L. Baskin and Co., Historical Publishers, 1881.

History of New Mexico: Its Resources and People, Illustrated. Vol. 1. Los Angeles: Pacific States, 1907.

Journal of the House of Representatives of the United States. Vol. 74. Washington, DC: Government Printing Office, 1874.

Journal of the House of Representatives of the United States. Vol. 75. Washington, DC: Government Printing Office, 1875.

Journal of the Senate of the State of Missouri at the Regular Session of the Twenty-Third General Assembly. Jefferson City: W. A. Curry, Public Printer, 1865.

Journal of the Senate of the United States of America. Vol. 70. Washington, DC: Government Printing Office, 1875.

Keleher, William A. *Maxwell Land Grant: A New Mexico Item.* Albuquerque: University of New Mexico Press, 1942.

Keleher, William A. *Violence in Lincoln County, 1869–1881, a New Mexico Item.* Albuquerque: University of New Mexico Press, 1957.

Lambert, Oscar Doane. *Stephen Benton Elkins.* Pittsburgh: University of Pittsburgh Press, 1955.

Lamm, Gene. *A Walking Tour of Old Town, Cimarron, New Mexico in the 1800s*. Cimarron, NM: Cimarron Historical Society, 2008.

Larson, Robert W. *New Mexico Populism: A Study of Radical Protest in a Western Territory*. Boulder: Colorado Associated University Press, 1974.

Larson, Robert W. *New Mexico's Quest for Statehood, 1846–1912*. Albuquerque: University of New Mexico Press, 1968.

MacDonald, Randall M., Gene Lamm, and Sarah E. MacDonald. *Images of America: Cimarron and Philmont. Charleston, SC: Arcadia, 2012*.

McDevitt, Kevin, with Ed Sitzberger. *History of the St. James Hotel, Cimarron, New Mexico*. Colorado Springs: Cimarron Press, 2019.

Message of Gov. Samuel B. Axtell to the Legislative Assembly of New Mexico, Twenty-second Session. Santa Fe, NM: Manderfield & Tucker, Public Printers, 1875.

Message of the President of the United States and Accompanying Documents to the Two Houses of Congress at the Commencement of the Third Session of the Fortieth Congress. Washington, DC: Government Printing Office, 1868.

Metz, Leon. *Border: The U.S.-Mexico Line*. Fort Worth: TCU Press, 2008.

Miller, Darlis A. *Open Range: The Life of Agnes Morley Cleaveland*. Norman: University of Oklahoma Press, 2010.

Mills, James B. *Billy the Kid:* El Bandido Simpático. Denton: University of North Texas Press, 2022.

Minutes of the Annual Conferences of the Methodist Episcopal Church for the Year 1872. New York: Nelson & Phillips, 1872.

Minutes of the Annual Conferences of the Methodist Episcopal Church for the Year 1876. New York: Nelson & Phillips, 1876.

Minutes of the New Mexico Bar Association, Fifth Annual Session, Together with Constitution and By-Laws as Amended and in Force January 31, 1890. Santa Fe: New Mexican Printing Company, 1890.

Miscellaneous Documents of the Senate of the United States for the Third Session of the Forty-fifth Congress, 1878–'79. Washington, DC: Government Printing Office, 1879.

Montoya, María. *Translating Property: The Maxwell Land Grant and the Conflict over Land in the American West, 1840–1900*. Berkeley: University of California Press, 2002.

Murphy, Lawrence R. *Philmont: A History of New Mexico's Cimarron County*. Albuquerque: University of New Mexico Press, 1972.

Nolan, Frederick. *The Lincoln County War: A Documentary History*. Norman: University of Oklahoma Press, 1992.

Nolan, Frederick. *Tascosa: Its Life and Gaudy Times*. Lubbock: Texas Tech University Press, 2007.

Nolan, Frederick. *The West of Billy the Kid*. Norman: University of Oklahoma Press, 1998.

O'Brien, Frank M. *The Story of The Sun*. New York: George H. Doran Company, 1918.

Oliva, Leo E. *Fort Union and the Frontier Army in the Southwest: A Historical Resource*. Santa Fe, NM: Division of History, National Park Service, 1993.

Palmquist, Peter E., and Thomas R. Kailbourn. *Pioneer Photographers from the Mississippi to the Continental Divide*. Stanford: Stanford University Press, 2005.

Parsons, Chuck. *Clay Allison: Portrait of a Shootist*. Seagraves, TX: Pioneer Book Publishers, 1983.

Pearson, Jim Berry. *The Maxwell Land Grant*. Norman: University of Oklahoma Press, 1961.

Perret, Geoffrey. *Ulysses S. Grant: Soldier and President*. New York: Random House, 1997.

Perrin, William Henry, ed. *History of Summit County, with an Outline Sketch of Ohio*. Chicago: Baskin & Battey, Historical Publishers, 1881.

Porter, Henry M. *Autobiography of Henry M. Porter*. Denver: Henry M. Porter, 1932.

Porter, Henry M. *Pencilings of an Early Western Pioneer*. Denver: World Press, 1929.

Prince, L. Bradford. *A Concise History of New Mexico*. Cedar Rapids: Torch Press, 1914.

Prince, L. Bradford. *The Student's History of New Mexico*. Denver: Publishers Press, 1921.

Proceedings of the American Society of Civil Engineers vol. 9 (January–December 1883).

Railroad Gazette: A Journal of Transportation, Engineering and Railroad News, Seventeenth Year. New York: Railroad Gazette, 1873.

Register of Officers and Agents, Civil, Military, and Naval, in the Service of the United States on the Thirtieth of September, 1875. Washington, DC: Government Printing Office, 1876.

Report of the Secretary of the Interior; Being Part of the Message and Documents Communicated to the Two Houses of Congress at the Beginning of the First Session of the Forty-Ninth Congress. Vol. 1. Washington, DC: Government Printing Office, 1885.

Rice, Allen Thorndike, ed. *The North American Review.* New York: North American Review, 1887.

Roberts, B. H. *A Comprehensive History of the Church of Jesus Christ of Latter-day Saints.* Vol. 5, *Century 1.* Provo: Brigham Young University Press, 1965.

Roster and Record of Iowa Soldiers in the War of the Rebellion. Vol. 2. Des Moines: Emory H. English, State Printer, 1908.

Serena, Louis F. *Clay Allison and the Colfax County War.* Albuquerque: Louis Serena, 2000.

Simon, John T., ed. *The Papers of Ulysses S. Grant.* Vol. 27. Carbondale: Southern Illinois University Press, 2005.

Siringo, Charles A. *Riata and Spurs: The Story of a Lifetime Spent in the Saddle as Cowboy and Detective.* Boston and New York: Houghton Mifflin, 1931.

Stanley, F. *The Elizabethtown, New Mexico Story.* Dumas, TX: F. Stanley, 1961.

Stanley, F. *The Grant That Maxwell Bought.* Denver: World Press, 1952.

Stanley, F. *Ike Stockton.* Denver: World Press, 1959.

Stanley, F. *Raton Chronicle.* Raton, NM: Coda, 2006.

Stout, Wayne. *History of Utah.* Vol. 1, *1870–1896.* Salt Lake City: Wayne Stout, 1907.

The Supreme Court Reporter. Vol. 7, *Cases Argued and Determined in the United States Supreme Court, October Term, 1886.* St. Paul: West Publishing Company, 1887.

The Supreme Court Reporter. Vol. 14, *Cases Argued and Determined in the United States Supreme Court, October Term, 1893.* St. Paul: West Publishing Company, 1894.

Taulbee, Rose A. *Taulbee: The History of the Taulbee Family in America.* Denver: Andrew Burt, 2006.

Taylor, Morris F. *O. P. McMains and the Maxwell Land Grant Conflict.* Tucson: University of Arizona Press, 1979.

Tibbles, Thomas Henry. *Buckskin and Blanket Days.* Garden City, NY: Doubleday & Company, 1957.

Transcript of Title of the Maxwell Land Grant Situated in New Mexico and Colorado. Chicago: Rand McNally, 1881.

Trow's New York City Directory, Volume XCII, for the Year Ending May 1, 1879. New York: Trow City Directory, 1879.

Twitchell, Ralph E. *Leading Facts of New Mexican History.* Vol. 2. Cedar Rapids: Torch Press, 1912.

United States Reports. Vol. 139, *Cases Adjudged in the Supreme Court at the October Term, 1890.* New York and Albany: Banks & Brothers, Law Publishers, 1891.

University of the State of New York: Eighty-Second Annual Report of the Regents of the University. Albany: Argus Company, Printers, 1869.

Utley, Robert M. *High Noon in Lincoln: Violence on the Western Frontier.* Albuquerque: University of New Mexico Press, 1987.

Van Nort, Sydney C. *The City College of New York.* Charleston: Arcadia, 2007.

Varney, Philip. *New Mexico's Best Ghost Towns: A Practical Guide.* Albuquerque: University of New Mexico Press, 1987.

Watrous, Ansel. *History of Larimer County Colorado.* Fort Collins: Courier Printing and Publishing, 1911.

Westphall, Victor. *Thomas Benton Catron and His Era.* Tucson: University of Arizona Press, 1973.

White, Koch, Kelley, and McCarthy, Attorneys at Law. *Land Title Study.* Santa Fe: New Mexico State Planning Office, 1971.

Wishart, David J., ed. *Encyclopedia of the Great Plains.* Lincoln: University of Nebraska Press, 2004.

Zimmer, Stephen, and Gene Lamm. *Images of America: Colfax County.* Charleston, SC: Arcadia, 2015.

Articles, Chapters, and Dissertations

"Ada McPherson Morley." *New Mexico Humanities Council*, accessed 2021. https://nmhumanities.org/NMwomen2020/SecondarySources/Suffrage%20NM%20Ada%20McPherson%20Morley.pdf

"Axtell, Samuel Beach (1819–1891)." *Biographical Directory of the United States Congress*, accessed 2011. http://bioguide.congress.gov/scripts/biodisplay.pl?index=A000349.

"Benjamin, Judah Philip (1811–1884)." *Biographical Directory of the United States Congress*, accessed 2008. http://bioguide.congress.gov/scripts/biodisplay.pl?index=b000365.

"Catron, Thomas Benton (1840–1921)." *Biographical Directory of the United States Congress*, accessed 2008. http://bioguide.congress.gov/scripts/biodisplay.pl?index=c000253.

Chamberlain, Kathleen P. "Billy the Kid, Susan McSween, Thomas Catron, and the Modernization of New Mexico, 1865–1912." Chap. 7 in *New Mexican Lives: Profiles and Historical Stories*, edited by Richard W. Etulain. Albuquerque: University of New Mexico Press, 2002.

"Cimarron," NewMexico.org, accessed 2022. https://www.newmexico. org/places-to-visit/regions/northeast/cimarron/.

Cleaveland, Norman. "The Great New Mexico Cover-Up: Frank Warner Angel's Reports." *Outlaw Gazette*, November 2000, p. 16.

Cunningham, Sharon. "The Allison Clan: A Visit." *Western-Outlaw Lawman Association Journal* (Winter 2003), 3–24.

Cunningham, Sharon. "Clay Allison: Good-Natured Holy Terror." *HistoryNet*, July 30, 2013. www.historynet.com/clay-allison-good-natured-holy-terror.htm.

"D&E History." *Davis & Elkins College*, accessed 2014. https://www.dewv. edu/de-info/de-history.

"Discover Cimarron, NM." CimarronNM.com, accessed 2022. http://www. cimarronnm.com.

"Elkins, Stephen Benton (1841–1911)." *Biographical Directory of the United States Congress*, accessed 2014. http://bioguide.congress.gov/scripts/ biodisplay.pl?index=E000110.

"Former Mayors of Santa Fe." Website of Santa Fe, NM, accessed 2014. www.santafenm.gov/mayors_of_santa_fe.

Freiberger, Harriet. "Lucien Maxwell: From Cimarron to Fort Sumner." *History Net*, March 1, 2017. http://www.historynet.com/lucien-maxwell-cimarron-fort-sumner.htm.

Haley, James L. "Red River War." *Handbook of Texas Online*, updated January 27, 2021. https://www.tshaonline.org/handbook/entries/red-river-war.

Hornung, Chuck. "The Forgotten Davy Crockett." *Quarterly of the National Association and Center for Outlaw and Lawman History* 13, no. 1 (Summer 1988): 8–13; 13, no. 2 (Fall 1988): 14–15.

"Isaac Wayne MacVeagh (1881): Attorney General." *UVA Miller Center*, accessed 2014. https://millercenter.org/president/arthur/essays/macveagh-1881-attorney-general.

"James Garfield." WhiteHouse.gov, accessed 2014. www.whitehouse.gov/1600/ presidents/jamesgarfield.

Jensen, Joan. "Disfranchisement Is a Disgrace: Women and Politics in New Mexico, 1900–1940." *New Mexico Historical Review* 56, no. 1 (1981): 5–35.

Kelsey, Harry E., Jr. "Clay Allison: Western Gunman." Chap. 16 in *1957 Brand Book of the Denver Westerners*, edited by Westerners Denver Posse. Boulder: Johnson, 1958.

Lamar, Howard R. "The Santa Fe Ring." Chap. 13 in Ellis, *New Mexico, Past and Present.*

Lowry, Sharon K. "Portrait of an Age: The Political Career of Stephen W. Dorsey, 1868–1899." PhD diss., University of North Texas, 1980. https://digital.library.unt.edu/ark:/67531/metadc332211/m2/1/high_res_d/1002783254-Lowry.pdf.

"Maxwell Shareholders Approve ABN AMRO, Dresdner Bid (Dutch)." *Bloomberg,* March 17, 2000. https://www.bloomberg.com/press-releases/2000-03-17/maxwell-shareholders-approve-abn-amro-dresdner-bid-dutch.

Newman, Simeon H., III. "The Santa Fe Ring: A Letter to the *New York Sun.*" *Arizona and the West* 12, no. 3 (Autumn 1970): 269–88.

"Panic of 1873." U-S-History.com, accessed 2010. http://www.u-s-history.com/pages/h213.html.

Pettit, R. F., Jr. "Maxwell Land Grant." In *Taos-Raton-Spanish Peaks Country (New Mexico and Colorado): New Mexico Geological Society 17th Annual Fall Field Conference Guidebook,* edited by S. A. Northrop and C. B. Read, 66–68. Socorro, NM: New Mexico Geological Society, 1966. https://nmgs.nmt.edu/publications/guidebooks/downloads/17/17_p0066_p0068.pdf.

Pierce, Michael D. "Red River War (1874–1875)." *Oklahoma Historical Society,* accessed 2021. https://www.okhistory.org/publications/enc/entry.php?entry=RE010.

Poldervaart, Arie. "Black-Robed Justice in New Mexico, 1846–1912." *New Mexico Historical Review* 22, no. 4 (1947): 351–88.

Recko, Corey. "Samuel B. Axtell and the Colfax County War: Axtell's 'Dear Ben' Letter." *Wild West History Association Journal* 2, no. 2 (April 2009): 43–52.

"Samuel Beach Axtell." *New Mexico History: State Records Center & Archives,* accessed 2018. http://newmexicohistory.org/people/samuel-beach-axtell.

Smith, Kristi. "S. H. Newman: Pioneer Newspaperman Fought Vice." *Borderlands* 22 (2003–2004). http://epcc.libguides.com/content.php?pid=309255&sid=2604083.

"Solicitor General: Samuel F. Phillips." *Office of the Solicitor General: US Department of Justice,* updated September 19, 2023. https://www.justice.gov/osg/bio/samuel-f-phillips.

Sonnichsen, C. L. "Allison, Robert Clay (1841–1887)." *Handbook of Texas Online,* updated November 1, 1994. www.tshaonline.org/handbook/online/articles/fal39.

"Springer Echinoderm Collection." *Smithsonian National Museum of National History,* accessed 2020. https://naturalhistory.si.edu/research/paleobiology/collections-overview/springer-echinoderm-collection.

Stanley, F. "O. P. McMains, Champion of a Lost Cause" *New Mexico Historical Review* 24 (January 1949): 1–11.

Stockton, Bill. "Clifton House." *New Mexico Magazine,* February 1963, 9–10.

Taylor, Morris F. "Plains Indians on the New Mexico–Colorado Border: The Last Phase, 1870–1876." *New Mexico Historical Review* 46, no. 4 (1971): 315–36.

Taylor, Morris F. "The Two Land Grants of Gervacio Nolán." *New Mexico Historical Review* 47, no. 2 (1972): 151–84.

"Union Major General Lew Wallace." *National Park Service: Monocacy National Battlefield, Maryland,* updated August 26, 2021. www.nps.gov/mono/historyculture/lewwallace.htm.

Weiser-Alexander, Kathy. "Elizabethtown: Gone but Not Forgotten." *Legends of America,* updated July 2023. http://www.legendsofamerica.com/nm-etown.html.

Wetherington, Mark V. "Ku Klux Klan." *Tennessee Encyclopedia,* accessed 2022. https://tennesseeencyclopedia.net/entries/ku-klux-klan/.

Wroth, William H. "Maxwell Land Grant." *New Mexico History: State Records Center & Archives,* accessed April 1, 2024. https://newmexicohistory.org/2014/09/15/maxwell-land-grant-d49/.

Collections, Archives, and Libraries

Archives of the City College of New York. City University of New York, NY.

Audrey Alpers Papers. New Mexico State University Archives and Special Collections, Las Cruces, NM.

Beaubien Family Photographs. Rio Grande Historical Collections. New Mexico State University Archives and Special Collections, Las Cruces, NM.

Bureau of Indian Affairs Letters Received. National Archives and Records Administration, College Park, MD.

Branson Library, New Mexico State University, Las Cruces, NM.

Brigham Young University Library, Provo, UT.

Case Western Reserve University Archives, Cleveland, OH.

Chuck Parsons's Clay Allison Papers (in author's collection), Hudson, OH.

Classified Photo Collection. Utah State Historical Society, Millcreek, UT.

Cleveland Public Library, Cleveland, OH.

Collis Potter Huntington Papers. Special Collections Research Center, Syracuse University Library, Syracuse, NY.

Dallas Public Library, Dallas, TX.

Western History Department, Denver Public Library, Denver, CO.

Donald S. Dreesen Collection of Pictures of Prominent New Mexicans. Center for Southwest Research. University of New Mexico, Albuquerque, NM.

Edgell (Ed) Gooden Collection, Albuquerque, NM.

El Paso Public Library, El Paso, TX.

Emerson Hough Papers, State Historical Society of Iowa, Des Moines, IA.

Eugene and Marilyn Glick Indiana History Center, Indiana Historical Society, Indianapolis, IN.

Frank Springer Papers. CS Cattle Company, Cimarron, NM.

Fred Lambert Papers. Center for Southwest Research. University of New Mexico, Albuquerque, NM.

General Records of the Department of Justice. National Archives and Records Administration, College Park, MD.

The Haley Memorial Library & History Center, Midland, TX.

Henn-Johnson Library and Local History Archives Foundation, Lincoln, NM.

Hudson Library and Historical Society, Hudson, OH.

Interior Department Appointment Papers. Territory of New Mexico, 1850–1907. National Archives and Records Administration, College Park, MD.

James Klaiber Collection, Lafayette, IN.

Kelvin Smith Library, Case Western Reserve University, Cleveland, OH.

Kent State University Library, Kent, OH.

Lakewood Public Library Main Library, Lakewood, OH.

Letters Received by Headquarters. District of New Mexico, September 1865–August 1890. National Archives and Records Administration, College Park, MD.

Lew Wallace Collection. William H. Smith Memorial Library. Indiana Historical Society, Indianapolis, IN.

Library of Congress Prints and Photographs Division. Library of Congress, Washington, DC.

Lionel Pincus and Princess Firyal Map Division. New York Public Library, New York, NY.

Longmont Museum, Longmont, CO.

Los Angeles Central Library, Los Angeles, CA.

Maxwell Land Grant Company Records. Center for Southwest Research. University of New Mexico, Albuquerque, NM.

Miguel Antonio Otero Photograph Collection. Center for Southwest Research. University of New Mexico, Albuquerque, NM.

Miscellaneous Manuscripts. Rutherford B. Hayes Presidential Center, Fremont, OH.

New Jersey State Archives, Department of State, Trenton, NJ.

New Mexico Annual Conference of the United Methodist Church Archives, Albuquerque, NM.

New Mexico State Records Center and Archives, Santa Fe, NM.

Newberry Library, Chicago, IL.

Norman Cleaveland Papers. Rio Grande Historical Collections. New Mexico State University Archives and Special Collections, Las Cruces, NM.

Old Aztec Mill Museum, Cimarron, NM.

Palace of the Governors Photo Archives, Santa Fe, NM.

Papers of Lew and Susan Wallace. William H. Smith Memorial Library. Indiana Historical Society, Indianapolis, IN.

Rush Rhees Library, University of Rochester, Rochester, NY.

State Historical Society of Iowa, Des Moines, IA.

TT Hagaman Southwest Collection. New Mexico Highlands University, Las Vegas, NM.

US Government Accountability Office, Washington, DC.

Victor Grant Collection Photo Albums. Arthur Johnson Memorial Library, Raton, NM.

West of the Pecos Museum, Pecos, TX.

William A. Keleher Collection. Center for Southwest Research. University of New Mexico, Albuquerque, NM.

William G. Ritch Collection. Huntington Library, San Marino, CA.

William H. Smith Memorial Library, Indiana Historical Society, Indianapolis, IN.

Wisconsin Veterans Museum, Madison, WI.

Zimmerman Library, University of New Mexico, Albuquerque, NM.

Zuhl Library, New Mexico State University, Las Cruces, NM.

Index

U

Uña de Gato grant, 99, 115
University of Missouri at Columbia, 18–19
Utah, 23–25, 93, 95–96, 127
Ute and Apache Indian Agency (Cimarron), 12

V

Vandiver House, Las Animas, Colorado, 91
Vega, Cruz, 38–40, 47–49, 51, 55–57, 60, 62–63, 68, 76, 84–85, 101–6, 121
Vermejo, New Mexico, 86–87

W

Waddingham, Wilson, 87
Wade, James F., 111
Waldo, Henry L., 34, 58, 67, 76, 81, 83, 85, 113
Wallace, Allen C., 148
Wallace, Lew, 124–25, 131–33, 135, 148
Wallace, Susan, 133
Waller, George, 47
Walz, Edgar, 19
Wapello, Iowa, 10
Washington, DC, 4, 9, 20, 25, 89, 91, 93–95, 142, 148–50, 165, 169
Watertown, New York, 115
Watkins, Erwin Curtis, 115
Watts, John S., 3
Wayne County, Tennessee, 44
Welding, Simeon Erastus, 49, 105
Western Reserve College, 23
Westport, Missouri, 18, 163
Whigham, Harry, 118, 148
Williams, Landaulet, 23, 169
Williamson, James A., 100, 150
Wilson, John B., 109
Winterset, Iowa, 7
Woods, George L., 24

Y

Young, Brigham, 24, 96–97